Contents

KU-769-129

An Invitation *Jeni Couzyn* 1

A Note on the Selection 6

Part One: Contemporary Poets

MUSE

Muse *Anna Akhmatova*, translated by *D. M. Thomas* 9
The Song of the Broken Reeds *Ingrid Jonker*,
   translated by *Jack Cope* and *William Plomer* 10
Invocation *Kathleen Raine* 11
The Child *P. K. Page* 12
The Mirage *Gwendolyn MacEwen* 13
Return from Arvon *Meg Easten* 14
Spell of Creation *Kathleen Raine* 15
   from Insomnia *Marina Tsvetayeva*, translated by
   Elaine Feinstein 17
from Poems for Blok *Marina Tsvetayeva*, translated by
   Elaine Feinstein 18
The World has Passed *Penelope Shuttle* 19
from Old Woman *Cam Hubert* 21

ENDS MEET

Ends Meet *Frances Bellerby* 27
All the Words *Gillian Hanscombe and Suniti Namjoshi* 29
Heart Note *Gillian Allnutt* 30
The Lion from Rio *Penelope Shuttle* 31
The Conceiving *Penelope Shuttle* 32
Giving Birth *Penelope Shuttle* 33
Praise Song for My Mother *Grace Nichols* 35
The Wound *Louise Glück* 36

In Celebration Of My Uterus *Anne Sexton*   38
A Vision *Denise Levertov*   41
Into the Hour *Elizabeth Jennings*   43
The Sleeper of the Rowan Tree *from* A Northumbrian
   Sequence *Kathleen Raine*   44

REMEMBER

Remember? *Alice Walker*   47
Wind a Change *Grace Nichols*   49
Kitchen Murder *Pat Lowther*   50
No Dialects Please *Merle Collins*   51
No Regrets *Patricia Hilaire*   54
Calderpark Zoo Song *Liz Lochhead*   56
Do a Dance for Daddy *Fran Landesman*   58
Rotting Song *Libby Houston*   59
Not Waving But Drowning *Stevie Smith*   60
Overheard in County Sligo *Gillian Clarke*   61
Egocentric *Stevie Smith*   62
Happiness *Stevie Smith*   63

THE FLAT EARTH

A Lecture to the Flat Earth Society
Gwendolyn MacEwen   64
The Surgeon at 2 a.m. *Sylvia Plath*   66
Watching Dark Circle *Denise Levertov*   68
Reading Hamlet *Anna Akhmatova*,
   translated by *D.M. Thomas*   69
Epilogue *from* Requiem *Anna Akhmatova*,
   translated by *D.M. Thomas*   70
Lot's Wife *Anna Akhmatova*,
   translated by *D.M. Thomas*   72
The Woman Who Wanted to be a Hero
   Michèle Roberts   73
Poem on the Day of the Autumn Equinox
   Michèle Roberts   75
Baby-Sitting *Gillian Clarke*   77

Singing
Down
the
Bones

Jeni Couzyn

First published by The Women's Press Limited 1989

A member of the Namara Group
34 Great Sutton Street, London EC1V 0DX

Copyright collection, notes and introduction © Jeni Couzyn 1989

British Library Cataloguing in Publication Data

Singing Down the Bones
  1. English poetry —
  I. Couzyn, Jeni, *1942–*
821′.914′08

  ISBN 0-7043-4130-1

Printed and bound in Great Britain by Hazell, Watson & Viney
Ltd, Aylesbury, Bucks.

The Woman Who Could Not Live With Her Faulty
    Heart *Margaret Atwood*   78
Some People's Dreams Pay All Their Bills
    Irina Ratushinskaya, translated by *David McDuff*   80
About Death *P.K. Page*   81

Part Two: Eminent Victorians

ELIZABETH BARRETT BROWNING
Romney's Proposal *from* Aurora Leigh   85

CHRISTINA ROSSETTI
Goblin Market   94

EMILY DICKINSON
A Selection   113

Part Three: Two Poems from Oral Traditions

The Charm of the Churn (Hebrides)
Recited by Mary Macleillan   120

The Story of Nangsa Obum (Tibet)
Told by Tsultrim Allione   125

Acknowledgements   135

An Invitation

'Where do poems come from?' This is a question I get asked often by people who have a feeling that they would like to write poems of their own. I usually answer that my poems come from somewhere deep within myself. But where is this mysterious, elusive, 'inside' place? How can one find it, walk about in it, go there looking for ideas? Practising poets know where the door is, although it's not an ordinary door. It's a series of doors, locked doors that open of their own accord under certain conditions. Sometimes poets go there when the conditions are right, knowing that they will find the door open for them when they arrive. At other times, when they are getting on with something quite different in their lives, a key will suddenly present itself. The key can be almost anything – an image, two words sparking together as they touch, or a particular sound . . . then the poet drops everything, rushes to the door, unlocks it with the key and scrambles inside to gather the treasure.

Well then, where is the door? If you would like to come with me, I will try to show you how to find it for yourself.

Begin by leaving behind everything you know about your external reality: your name, where you live, what you look like – everything.

You are in a house. It is completely empty, and completely silent. You don't see anything, or hear anything. You are quite still in the feeling of being yourself, alive.

If you can achieve this, even for a moment, you've begun your journey.

In a moment you are going to go *outside* and explore that space which you normally think of as the world

inside your head – not the streets and landscapes
your body normally inhabits, but a world that
represents your mind and feelings as you are now, at
this moment.

As you sit in the stillness, you become aware of
thoughts tugging you outwards. Allow yourself to be
drawn out. You are outside the house, in a garden, your
garden. Imagine your thoughts are this garden. There
are beds of flowers, vines, trees, pathways, a lawn. Each
growing thing represents a thought, or an area of
thought in your mind. The things you like to think
about are bright flowers. You planted them, tended
them, fed them, watched them grow. Or perhaps a
certain subject is an enormous tree. A fruit tree. You
climb it to gather fruit. You water it when the weather
is dry. You keep it free of caterpillars. Another subject
may be a fish pond. On certain days it is still and clear.
It reflects the sky. Goldfish are visible swimming about.
On other days it is murky and opaque, with dead leaves
and bits of rubbish floating on the surface.

You are in control here, you are the gardener. Everything in this part of your mind is a reflection of your
effort. Yet weeds, the thoughts you don't like, are
always there as well. The things you worry about – the
angry or sorrowful conversations that go on and on in
your head – although you try to clear them out of your
garden, they always come back. Where do they come
from? The seeds are waiting under the earth and begin
to sprout again at the first opportunity. You are
tangling with knots of brambles that tear your arms as
you try to root them out. These are those vigorous,
determined thoughts like jealousy, or old resentments
that are so hard to get rid of.

Walk about in your garden for a while, looking at it
all. Name the plants, the flourishing areas, the neglected
areas. Look at your ideas growing around you, the

things you like to think about, and remember, and understand.

One of them might be an idea for a poem – an image that you like, or the sound of a small string of words. Jot it down.

Now you notice that there is a gate in the garden wall. You push, and it opens quite easily. Step outside into the next level of your mind, taking your idea with you.

This is the wild country. It represents your personal experience. Imagine everything that happens to you as an aspect of nature. Perhaps your world feels like a desert, or is mountainous and steep, or full of dangerous mud-swamps and quicksand. On the other hand perhaps it is wide green fields, rolling hills. Imagine yourself in this landscape. You are less in control here than you were in your garden. Here you endure or enjoy the landscape in which you find yourself. Think of your relationships, for example. Being close to a friend might be represented by walking in a benign valley. But perhaps the friend turns away from you, or someone you love dies, or there is a war in your country, or you become ill. Now the landscape changes: a thick mist comes down over the valley, and suddenly it is frightening, malevolent. A gentle hillside turns into steep slopes of loose shingle. The earth drops away at your feet.

Things happen to you here which you can't choose, but you can choose the direction you walk in. You can decide to hide, or run, or lie down and go to sleep. What is your wild country like, today, at this moment? Explore it, be in it for a while and watch yourself in it. This is where the idea that formed in your garden takes on its body and colour. Words and sentences of your poem begin to run together and take form.

You may not want to go further. You may want to

stay in your wild country until your poem is written, and then return to your garden, where you use your knowledge of language to tidy up and complete your poem.

For those who want to go further, there is another territory beyond the wild country. It is ocean territory – the hardest of all to enter.

When you enter ocean territory you enter that part of the mind sometimes called the unconscious, where you have even less control than you had in the wild country. This is the world of dream and myth and archetype. In this watery space everything is joined to everything else. Time is not linear, but all around you. The ocean has always been there – the same ocean that nourishes the land and is fed by the rivers and streams. Water rises from the ocean, and rain falls. The waters are under the earth and above the earth. The waters are flowing in the veins and capillaries of all things living. Here you find the true centre of your poem – that point at which what is true for you is also true for other people not because your experience is vague and abstract, but because you are seeing *through* ordinary things as if they were transparent.

You have surrendered all attempts to be the director here. You can do nothing against the huge waters. You are carried on the back of a wave as if you were a dust-mote. The best you can do here is try to remain awake, observing and recording.

The poems that have reached ocean territory are universal, because they have transcended the boundaries of personal experience.

Sometimes the ocean rushes at the land in a tidal wave. In poetry this is called inspiration. These are the poems that seem to come all by themselves, complete and satisfying. Always the poet feels a sense of wonder with these rather precious and rare poems – as if they were written by someone else.

More often, though, it is necessary to travel the long way to ocean territory, and to accept that it will not often be possible to reach it. When you have travelled as far as you can on your journey, you take your poem notes and return to your garden, the place of intellect and learned knowledge and ideas. Here you look at what you have written with a critical eye. You tidy up the rhythms and cut away the dead branches. You search out the clichés and burn them. You give your poem a title and put it away for a while to see whether it disintegrates like fairy money, or is still a poem when you look at it again.

Now you leave your garden and enter your house. Your empty house. Sit down and close your eyes. It is quiet. Nothing moves. Your breath drops in, out, in, out, without effort. It is completely dark in your house, but you don't need to see anything. You are utterly still. The walls of your house seem to be retreating. Your house is wide, deep. It seems to fill a vast space. Slowly you become aware of the stars. They are in your house, millions of miles within your house. You don't see them with your eyes, yet you see them as if your eyes had just been made. You would like to stay like this for ever.

That thought of for ever flings the windows open – you hear traffic sounds, the birds twittering, somewhere a telephone ringing. A robust wind is tugging you back. You are in the world again.

You haven't got a poem to show for this last past of your journey, but you feel lighter, more joyful. Next time you try to write a poem it will be a little easier.

Why not try it now? What is your garden like? Your wild country? Your ocean territory?

Have the bones been cast for you?

Sing them down. Sing them down with your poem

and all the poems of women who would not accept the narrow territory the bone-man cast for them. Sing your poems down the arteries and the veins, down into the heart, sing the poems down into the stars inside your empty, still house. Singing down the bones, set off on your journey.

Jeni Couzyn
London, March 1989

A Note on the Selection

Unlike those editors who claim to have read 'everything' and put together an anthology that represents 'the best of its kind' I make no such claims. I don't think of poetry as something with a value that can be fixed and calculated.

I believe that the response of an individual to a poem is an organic thing. Energy is needed both from the poem and the individual reading it, for the magic to happen. The two energies meet, something changes, the poem has worked. Or they don't meet, and the poem has failed. The energy that a reader brings to a poem depends on the state of that person's consciousness at the time – a fluid and changeable thing. It is not governed by an acquired knowledge of poetic technique, or a set of learned responses. There is a great deal one can usefully learn about how to read poetry, but in the end, when a poem *works*, it transcends both lesson and poet, and takes on a life of its own in the heart of the reader.

All the poems in this collection are alive in me now, as I arrange them here. I've gathered them as one might gather singers for a group, with one ear on the individual voice, and one on the collective sound.   JC

Part One
Contemporary Poets

Most of the poets in part one are alive and writing in 1988. The exceptions are:

Anna Akhmatova, Stevie Smith, and Frances Bellerby who died in 1966, 1971, and 1975 respectively;
and Maria Tsvetayeva (d.1941), Sylvia Plath (d.1963), Ingrid Jonker (d.1965), Anne Sexton (d.1974), Pat Lowther (d.1975), and Gwendolyn MacEwen (d.1988), whose lives ended prematurely under tragic circumstances.

The poems are arranged in four movements:

MUSE

ENDS MEET

REMEMBER

THE FLAT EARTH

MUSE

Muse

When at night I wait for her to come,
Life, it seems, hangs by a single strand.
What are glory, youth, freedom, in comparison
With the dear welcome guest, a flute in hand?

She enters now. Pushing her veil aside,
She stares through me with her attentiveness.
I question her: 'And were you Dante's guide,
Dictating the Inferno?' She answers: 'Yes.'

Anna Akhmatova,
translated by *D. M. Thomas*

The Song of the Broken Reeds

The wind from the Torwana mountains
has her lap full of moss
She carries a sleeping child
she recites from the stars
with the voice of broad waters
against the white skeleton of the day

The wind from the Torwana mountains
shoreless without horizon without seasons
has the face of all people
has the bitter-aloe of the world at her breast
has the lamb of all joy over her shoulder
and the hangman of every daybreak in her eyes

The wind from the Torwana mountains
with her lap full of moss
carries a sleeping child
carries a night of thistles
carries a death without darkness

and blows through the broken reeds

Ingrid Jonker
translated by *Jack Cope* and *William Plomer*

Invocation

There is a poem on the way,
there is a poem all round me,
the poem is in the near future,
the poem is in the upper air
above the foggy atmosphere
it hovers, a spirit
that I would make incarnate.
Let my body sweat
let snakes torment my breast
my eyes be blind, ears deaf, hands distraught
mouth parched, uterus cut out,
belly slashed, back lashed,
tongue slivered into thongs of leather
rain stones inserted in my breasts,
head severed,

if only the lips may speak,
if only the god will come.

Kathleen Raine

The Child

I dreamed the child was dead
and folded in a box
like stockings or a dress.

I dreamed its toys and games
its brightly-coloured clothes
were lying on the grass

and with them I was left
adult and dutiful
with ink instead of blood.

I could not bear the grief
accommodate the loss –
as if my heart had died.

On wakening I saw
the child beside my bed
Not dead! not dead! I cried.

But startled by my voice
and fearful of my glance
the phantom infant fled.

P. K. Page

The Mirage

This is the desert, as I promised you.
        There are no landmarks, only
Those you imagine, or those made by rocks
        that fell from heaven.

Did you ever know where you were going?
        Am I as invisible to you
As you always were to me, fellow traveller?
        You are not here for nothing.

There are no easy ways of seeing, riding
        the waves of invisible seas
In marvellous vessels which are always
        arriving or departing.

I have come to uncover the famous secrets
        of earth and water, air and fire.
I have come to explore and contain them all.
        I am an eye.

I need tons of yellow space, and nothing
        in the spectrum is unknown to me.
I am the living centre of your sight; I draw for you
        this thin and dangerous horizon.

Gwendolyn MacEwen

Return from Arvon

Dusting, your face on the cover of a book reminded me:
just the other day, words took my breath away.
Now they call children out of the rain.
Hands, through which my bird flew in translation,
Pound the grey out of white socks into my eyes.
Books and paper have become something to touch and
        smell and put away.
This pen, that crossed out words like 'infinite soul'
and wrote words so right I can't remember them,
writes – fish fingers
                washing powder
                apples
                crisps
                cat food
                bubble bath.

Meg Easten

Spell of Creation

Within the flower there lies a seed,
Within the seed there springs a tree,
Within the tree there spreads a wood.

In the wood there burns a fire,
And in the fire there melts a stone,
Within the stone a ring of iron.

Within the ring there lies an O
Within the O there looks an eye,
In the eye there swims a sea,

And in the sea reflected sky,
And in the sky there shines the sun,
Within the sun a bird of gold.

Within the bird there beats a heart,
And from the heart there flows a song,
And in the song there sings a word.

In the word there speaks a world,
A word of joy, a world of grief,
From joy and grief there springs my love.

Oh love, my love, there springs a world,
And on the world there shines a sun
And in the sun there burns a fire,

Within the fire consumes my heart
And in my heart there beats a bird,
And in the bird there wakes an eye,

Within the eye, earth, sea and sky,
Earth, sky and sea within an O
Lie like the seed within the flower.

Kathleen Raine

from Insomnia

In my enormous city it is   night,
as from my sleeping house I go   out,
and people think perhaps I'm a daughter or wife
but in my mind is one thought only   night.

The July wind now sweeps a way for   me,
From somewhere, some window, music though   faint.
The wind can blow until the dawn   today,
in through the fine walls of the breast rib-cage.

Black poplars, windows, filled with   light.
Music from high buildings, in my hand a flower.
Look at my steps   following   nobody
Look at my shadow, nothing's here of me.

The lights   are like threads of golden beads
in my mouth is the taste of the night   leaf.
Liberate me from the bonds of   day,
my friends, understand: I'm nothing but your dream.

Marina Tsvetayeva,
translated by *Elaine Feinstein*

from Poems for Blok

Your name is a   bird in my hand
a piece of   ice on the tongue
one single movement of the lips.
Your name is: five signs,
a ball caught in flight, a
silver bell in the mouth

a stone, cast in a quiet pool
makes the splash of your name, and
the sound is in the clatter of
night hooves, loud as a thunderclap
or it speaks straight into my forehead,
shrill as the click of a cocked gun.

Your name   how impossible, it
is a kiss in the eyes on
motionless eyelashes, chill and sweet.
Your name is a kiss of snow,
a gulp of icy spring water, blue
as a dove. About your name is: sleep.

Marina Tsvetayeva,
translated by *Elaine Feinstein*

The World has Passed*

On the other side of the rose
there is the felling of trees

On the other side of the frost
there is the colour of a bruise

On the other side of the ovum
there is the woman of warfare

On the other side of the bonfire
there is the music springing back,
the retaliation

On the other side of the leaf
is the lesson in lacemaking

On the other side of the room
is a cabinet of curiosities, antique granary

On the other side of the mother
is a sigh full of filaments,
a few words walking on tiptoe

On the other side of the blackberry
is the harvest of the moon

On the other side of the voice
is the absence of the waterfall

On the other side of the ice
is the half-satisfied sea

On the other side of the blood
is the unrooted child

On the other side of the child
is the gulping-down of cloud,
the whispering of loopholes –
arrival at last at the fresh shrine

Penelope Shuttle

*Yokut. Native American term for
'a year has gone by'.

from Old Woman

i
From the eye of the raven
Old Woman came

From the mind of the eagle
Old Woman came

From the heart of the heron
Old Woman came

From within the oyster shell
Old Woman came

From the fin of the salmon
Old Woman came

From the mouth of the halibut
Old Woman came

From the tooth of the whale
Old Woman came

From the belly of Old Woman
this one came

iii
Old Woman knew and her skin split
she came renewed from her old shell
the odour of her own decay
rising like smoke, dying like fire

She saw in her new self
traces of the old
she watched a man's face
become shadowed wrinkles
and she knew; man could never
be renewed
without her

Old Woman lives within herself
keeping her own council when
words flow too fast
and young souls forget the truth

She lives within herself
her memories swelling, waiting
for the time she knows and
her skin splits

inside her skin she is alone
but never lonely

v
At night an old woman
rises from the sea
clutching her bones become a broom
she sweeps the sand

At night an old woman
moves through sedge grass
searching souls for her basket
and tears to quench her thirst

At night an old woman
becomes a warm blanket
you lie on it and while you sleep
she becomes pregnant

In the morning you are gone
She is renewed
goes back to the sea
you live forever within her

vi
She calls and the ravens answer
leading you always to sweet water
which you can follow to the sea
so you are never lost

She calls and the cormorants hear
skimming across the wave-tips
moving always toward fish
so you are never hungry

She calls and flowers ride
on the wind of her breath
She laughs and the lakes fill
so you are never thirsty

She calls and creation answers
You are found and fed, you
sleep beside your love
so you are never cold

She calls and you hear
become like the cormorant
once blind and lost, now part
of the perfection of her call

viii
Old Woman knows
the weeping of the barren womb
Old Woman knows

Old Woman knows
the demanding heat become ashes
Old Woman knows

Old Woman knows
the scent and feel of fear
Old Woman knows

Old Woman knows
the eyes staring from the ocean floor
Old Woman knows

when all the men are talking
when all the men are foolish
when all the men are drinking
telling lies and spitting

Old Woman walks to the beach
leaving them to their games

Old Woman knows
they would use her if she would let them

Old Woman knows
they want her because they are lazy

Old Woman knows
she leaves them to their games

xiv
A century ago your touch
shook the dream rattle,
the daemons fled, awed by
a woman happy in her nakedness.
Raven laughed perched atop the magic box
where once the moon was stored

That summer had us dancing
naked in the long grass

At night we moved in rhythm on the bed
the hours passing like herons in flight

In pine scent with roses
we walked the riverbank laughing

Tonight the bed is half empty
the moments ticking the endless night
and on the beach the heron
stands with his eyes
closed

xv
Old Woman help me
that one has torn me
he has entered me
left someone inside me
eating my head
bleeding me

bruising me
with lies

Old Woman become me
fill my bones
fill my veins
fill my eyes
that I not thirst
or burn
or fear

Cam Hubert

ENDS MEET

Ends Meet

My grandmother came down the steps into the garden.
She shone in the gauzy air.
She said: 'There an old woman at the gate –
See what she wants, my dear.'

My grandmother's eyes were blue like the damsels
Darting and swerving above the stream,
Or like the kingfisher arrow shot into darkness
Through the archway's dripping gleam.

My grandmother's hair was silver as sunlight.
The sun had been poured right over her, I saw,
And ran down her dress and spread a pool for her
    shadow
To float in. And she would live for evermore.

There was nobody at the gate when I got there.
Not even a shadow hauling along the road,
Nor my yellow snail delicate under the ivy,
Nor my sheltering cold-stone toad.

But the sunflowers aloft were calm. They'd seen no one.
They were sucking light, for ever and a day.
So I busied myself with going away unheeded
And with having nothing to say.

No comment, nothing to tell, or to think,
Whilst the day followed the homing sun.
There was no old woman at my grandmother's gate.

And there isn't at mine.

Frances Bellerby

All the words

All the words have leaped into air like the cards
in Alice, like birds flying, forming, re-
forming, swerving and rising, and each word
says it is love. The cat says it is love.
It says, 'I am and I love.' And the fawn
in the forest who lost his name, he eats
from your hand. He tells you, 'My name is love.'
And all the White Knight's baggage rattles, and cries
it is love. And even the tiger-lily, even the rose
say only that they are themselves. And they say
they are love. All the little words say
they are love, the space in between, the link
and logic of love. And I can make no headway
in this heady grammar, and suddenly
and here, you are, I am, and we love.

Gillian Hanscombe
Suniti Namjoshi

heart note

because we for a while had been living there my heart

thought it was a house with cupboards and an open fire
and a door giving onto
an impossible steep twisted stair my heart

thought it could have small uncurtained windows it
    could go on
being there under its tiles for the swallows
every year

love was already living in the house my heart

thought when we got there it thought it was
a letterbox a back door opening to
a garden it could walk in

it was nothing we had put there but before us it was

apple willow and a wilderness of
rose thorn thick and dark
and light with its daylong delicate flowers my heart

thought it had roots it thought it could cover its roots
with straw it thought it could carry on
lighting its every morning fire

because we as love for a while had been living there

Gillian Allnutt

The Lion from Rio

Golden inclination
of the huge maned head
as he rests against my knee,
his massiveness like feathers against me
amid this Rio crowd
through which he came to me,
this lion, my lion,
my lion of lifelong light,
padding unnoticed through the carnival.
Now his beast head rests in my lap,
golden flood, I am laden with it.
Looking up at me with his gentle puzzled gaze,
he says helplessly, but I am a man, a man!

My own child could have told me.
He was a man.
How could I not have seen it?
Listen again, he is drowsily moaning,
I am a man.

Penelope Shuttle

The Conceiving

Now
you are in the ark of my blood
in the river of my bones
in the woodland of my muscles
in the ligaments of my hair
in the wit of my hands
in the smear of my shadow
in the armada of my brain
under the stars of my skull
in the arms of my womb
Now you are here
you worker in the gold of flesh

Penelope Shuttle

Giving Birth

Delivering this gift
requires blood,
a remote room,
the presence of overseers.

They tug a child
out of the ruins of your flesh.

Birth is not given.
It is what is taken from you;
not a gift you give
but a tax levied on you.

Not a gift but a bout
that ages both the contestants.

Birthshocks hold on tight, for years,
like hooked bristles of goosegrass,
cleavers clinging to your skirt and sleeves.

The raw mime of labour
is never healed,
in giving birth
the woman's innocence goes,
loss you can't brush away,
it stains all your new clothes.

No longer can you be half-woman, half-bird.
Now you are all woman,
you are all given away,
your child has the wings,
can resist the pull of the earth.

34

You watch her rush up,
clowning her way through the cloud.

And you applaud.

Penelope Shuttle

Praise Song for My Mother

You were
water to me
deep and bold and fathoming

You were
moon's eye to me
pull and grained and mantling

You were
sunrise to me
rise and warm and streaming

You were
the fishes red gill to me
the flame tree's spread to me
the crab's leg/the fried plantain smell
                    replenishing replenishing

Go to your wide futures, you said

Grace Nichols

The Wound

The air stiffens to a crust.
From bed I watch
Clots of flies, crickets
Frisk and titter. Now
The weather is such grease.
All day I smell the roasts
Like presences. You
Root into your books.
You do your stuff.
In here my bedroom walls
Are paisley, like a plot
Of embryos. I lie here,
Waiting for its kick.
My love. My tenant.
As the shrubs grow
Downy, bloom and seed.
The hedges grow downy
And seed and moonlight
Burbles through the gauze.
Sticky curtains. Faking scrabble
With the pair next door
I watched you clutch your blank.
They're both on Nembutal,
The killer pill.

And I am fixed. Gone careful,
Begging for the nod,
You hover loyally above my head. I close
My eyes. And now
The prison falls in place:
Ripe things sway in the light,
Parts of plants, leaf
Fragments . . .
You are covering the cot
With sheets. I feel
No end. No end. It stalls
In me. It's still alive.

Louise Glück

In Celebration Of My Uterus

Everyone in me is a bird.
I am beating all my wings.
They wanted to cut you out
but they will not.
They said you were immeasurably empty
but you are not.
They said you were sick unto dying
but they were wrong.
You are singing like a school girl.
You are not torn.

Sweet weight,
in celebration of the woman I am
and of the soul of the woman I am
and of the central creature and its delight
I sing for you. I dare to live.
Hello, spirit. Hello, cup.
Fasten, cover. Cover that does contain.
Hello to the soil of the fields.
Welcome, roots.

Each cell has a life.
There is enough here to please a nation.
It is enough that the populace own these goods.
Any person, any commonwealth would say of it,
"It is good this year that we may plant again
and think forward to a harvest.
A blight had been forecast and has been cast out."
Many women are singing together of this:
one is in a shoe factory cursing the machine,
one is at the aquarium tending a seal,
one is dull at the wheel of her Ford,
one is at the toll gate collecting,
one is tying the cord of a calf in Arizona,
one is straddling a cello in Russia,
one is shifting pots on the stove in Egypt,
one is painting her bedroom walls moon colour,
one is dying but remembering a breakfast,
one is stretching on her mat in Thailand,
one is wiping the ass of her child,
one is staring out the window of a train
in the middle of Wyoming and one is
anywhere and some are everywhere and all
seem to be singing, although some can not
sing a note.

Sweet weight,
in celebration of the woman I am
let me carry a ten-foot scarf,
let me drum for the nineteen-year-olds,
let me carry bowls for the offering
(if that is my part).
Let me study the cardiovascular tissue,
let me examine the angular distance of meteors,
let me suck on the stems of flowers
(if that is my part).
Let me make certain tribal figures
(if that is my part).
For this thing the body needs
let me sing
for the supper,
for the kissing,
for the correct
yes.

Anne Sexton

A Vision

*'The intellectual love of a thing is the
understanding of its perfections.'*
Spinoza, quoted by Ezra Pound

Two angels among the throng of angels
paused in the upward abyss,
facing angel to angel.

Blue and green glowed the wingfeathers
of one angel, from red to gold the sheen
of the other's. These two,

so far as angels may dispute, were poised
on the brink of dispute, brink of
fall from angelic stature,

for these tall ones, angels
whose wingspan encompasses entire
earthly villages, whose heads if their feet touched earth

would top pines or redwoods, live by their vision's
    harmony
which sees at one glance
the dark and light of the moon.

These two hovered dazed before one another,
for one saw the seafeathered, peacock breakered
crests of the other angel's magnificence,
different from his own,

and the other's eyes flickered with vision of
flame petalling, cream-gold grainfeather glitterings,
the wings of his fellow,

and both in immortal danger of dwindling, of dropping
into the remote forms of a lesser being.

But as these angels, the only halted ones
among the many who passed and repassed,
trod air as swimmers tread water, each gazing

on the angelic wings of the other,
the intelligence proper to great angels flew into their
   wings,
the intelligence called *intellectual love*, which,
understanding the perfections of scarlet,

leapt up among blues and greens strongshafted,
and among amber down illumined the sapphire bloom,

so that each angel was iridescent with the strange
   newly-seen
hues he watched; and their discovering pause
and the speech their silent interchange of perfection was

never became a shrinking to opposites,

and they remained free in the heavenly chasm,
remained angels, but dreaming angels,
each imbued with the mysteries of the other.

Denise Levertov

Into the Hour

I have come into the hour of a white healing.
Grief's surgery is over and I wear
The scar of my remorse and of my feeling.

I have come into a sudden sunlit hour
When ghosts are scared to corners. I have come
Into the time when grief begins to flower

Into a new love. It had filled my room
Long before I recognized it. Now
I speak its name. Grief finds its good way home.

The apple-blossom's handsome on the bough
And Paradise spreads round. I touch its grass.
I want to celebrate but don't know how.

I need not speak though everyone I pass
Stares at me kindly. I would put my hand
Into their hands. Now I have lost my loss

In some way I may later understand.
I hear the singing of the summer grass.
And love, I find, has no considered end,

Nor is it subject to the wilderness
Which follows death. I am not traitor to
A person or a memory. I trace

Behind that love another which is running
Around, ahead. I need not ask its meaning.

Elizabeth Jennings

The Sleeper of the Rowan Tree
from A Northumbrian Sequence

The sleeper at the rowan's foot
Dreams the darkness at the root,
Dreams the flow that ascends the vein
And fills with world the dreamer's brain.

Wild tree filled with wind and rain
Day and night invade your dream,
Unseen brightness of the sun,
Waters flowing underground
Rise in bud and flower and shoot;
And the burden is so great
Of the dark flow from without,
Of sun streaming from the sky
And the dead rising from the root,
Of the earth's desire to be
In this dreaming incarnate
That world has overflowed the tree.

Oh do not wake, oh do not wake
The sleeper in the rowan's shade,
Mountains rest within his thought,
Clouds are drifting in his brain,
Snows upon his eyelids fall,
Winds are piping in his song,
Night is gathered at his root,
Stars are blossoming in his crown,
Storm without finds peace within,
World is resting in his dream.

Lonely dreamer on the hill
I have dreamed a thousand years,
I have dreamed returning spring,
Earth's delight and golden sun,
I have dreamed the pheasant's eye,
The heather and the flashing burn,
For the world has filled my dream:
Dream has overflowed the tree.

World without presses so sore
Upon the roots and branches fine
The dreamer can contain no more
And overflows in falling flowers,
Lets fall the bitter rowan fruit
Harsh as tears and bright as blood,
Berries that the wild birds eat
Till stripped of dream the sleeper lies,
Stripped of world the naked tree.
But on the hillside I have heard
The voice of the prophetic bird
That feeds upon the bitter fruit,
I have heard the blackbird sing
The wild music of the wind,
Utter the note the sun would cry,
Sing for the burn that flows away.

The sleeper of the rowan tree
As full of earth as dream can know,
As full of dream as tree can bear
Sends the bird singing in the air
As full of world as song can cry,
And yet the song is overflowed,
For pressing at the tree's deep root
Still underground, unformed, is world.
The invading world must break the dream
So heavy is the weight of sky,
So violent the water's flow
So vast the hills that would be born,
Beyond the utterance of bird
The mountain voice that would be sung,
The world of wild that would be man:
The dream has overflowed the tree.

Kathleen Raine

REMEMBER

Remember?

Remember me?
I am the girl
with the dark skin
whose shoes are thin
I am the girl
with rotted teeth
I am the dark
rotten-toothed girl
with the wounded eye
and the melted ear.

I am the girl
holding their babies
cooking their meals
sweeping their yards
washing their clothes
Dark and rotting
and wounded, wounded.

I would give
to the human race
only hope.

I am the woman
with the blessed
dark skin
I am the woman
with teeth repaired
I am the woman
with the healing eye
the ear that hears.

I am the woman: Dark,
repaired, healed
Listening to you.

I would give
to the human race
only hope.

I am the woman
offering two flowers
whose roots
are twin

Justice and Hope

Let us begin.

Alice Walker

Wind a Change

Wind a change
blow soft but
steadfast

ripple the spears
of sugar cane
stir slow the leaves
of indigo

Dance
waltz
soothe
this old mud-wattle
hut
bring if you can
the smell of Dahomey
again

Wind a change
cool mountain water
open river flower

But pass easy
up the big house
way
let them sleep
they happy white sleep

Yes, Wind a change
keep yuh coming fire
secret

Grace Nichols

Kitchen Murder

Everything here's a weapon:
i pick up a meat fork,
imagine
plunging it in,
a heavy male
thrust

in two hands
i heft a stone-
ware plate, heavy
enough?

rummage the cupboards:
red pepper, rape-
seed oil, Drano

i'll wire myself
into a circuit:
the automatic perc,
the dishwasher, the
socket above the sink

i'll smile an electric
eel smile:
whoever touches
me is dead.

Pat Lowther

No Dialects Please

In this competition
dey was lookin for poetry of worth
for a writin that could wrap up a feelin
an fling it back hard
with a captive power to choke de stars
so dey say,
'Send them to us
but NO DIALECTS PLEASE'
We're British!

Ay!
Well ah laugh till me boushet near drop
Is not only dat ah tink
of de dialect of de Normans and de Saxons
dat combine an reformulate
to create a language-elect
is not only dat ah tink
how dis British education mus really be narrow
if it leave dem wid no knowledge
of what dey own history is about
is not only dat ah tink
bout de part of my story
dat come from Liverpool in a big dirty white ship
mark
AFRICAN SLAVES PLEASE!
We're the British!

But as if dat not enough pain
for a body to bear
ah tink bout de part on de plantations down dere
Wey dey so frighten o de power
in the deep spaces
behind our watching faces
dat dey shout
NO AFRICAN LANGUAGES PLEASE!
It's against the law!
Make me ha to go
an start up a language o me own
dat ah could share wid me people

Den when we start to shout
bout a culture o we own
a language o we own
a identity o we own
dem an de others dey leave to control us say
STOP THAT NONSENSE NOW
We're all British!
Every time we lif we foot to do we own ting
to fight we own fight
dey tell us how British we British
an ah wonder if dey remember
dat in Trinidad in the thirties
dey jail Butler
who dey say is their British citizen
an accuse him of
Hampering the war effort!
Then it was
FIGHT FOR YOUR COUNTRY, FOLKS!
You're British!

Ay! Ay!
Ah wonder when it change to
NO DIALECTS PLEASE!
WE'RE British!
Huh!
To tink how still dey so dunce
an so frighten o we power
dat dey have to hide behind a language
that we could wrap roun we little finger
in addition to we own!
Heavens o mercy!
Dat is dunceness oui!
Ah wonder where is de bright British?

Merle Collins

No Regrets

'Hay brown girl
wit yu woman liba ways
don't forget yu culture
black yu is black
now how you feel bout dat
yu can't pretend yu white
yu should know by now, dat ain't right
all we want is yu loyalty to de race
support yu brothers
we dont want yu white feminist ways'

So brother, afraid of my black feminist ways?
Afraid of my vocal range?
It's alright to fight the race war
when we dealing with the white racist
but when we get together, race becomes
second in line to the black sister
and our womanism takes the first place.

'Yu can't go on like dat sister
we hev to pull together
a woman mus stan by her man side
yu going on like yu wan fight me
bout womanism
next you'll be telling me bout
lesbianism.'

Listen, if I wan to stand by anybody side
please let me hev the choice.

'But tell me, is wha goin happen when yu
wan a sweet dance?
Yu going wan me den.'

No, not really.
You see, if I want to rock to the soul
or groove to jazz funk
my sister will join me, so leave the floor.
Oh, you think when the lovers rock hit the floor
I going to want you?
Well you jus watch how we hold the floor.

'Gowan wit yu woman ways
see how far yu getting without me . . .
wotless bitch!'

Think of your approach
you don't own me
and na bother raise yu hand fe hit me
cause you never born me!!

'Yu black woman go-wan
yu is devisive . . .
yu ah go regret it . . .
'cause yu can't manage widout me . . .'

It's true you don't know
and is a pity you don't know . . .
why you don't jus stop there and
watch, see how we manage
widout you . . .

Patricia Hilaire

Calderpark Zoo Song

Wir nocturnals are insomniac
And canny sleep till dark –
A' us animals are crackers,
Here in Calderpark.

Oor dromedary's plenty duende,
Wir porcupine's been in the wars,
Oor zebra's got zero libido –
He kerries aroon
His ain prison baurs.

Aw bit, naw bit, yiv goat the wrang
Orangutang –
Aw bit, naw bit
Oor orangutang's goat Angst.

The introverted ostrich hates
The manic marmoset
And oor ibex is
A nervous wreck, she's
Constantly under the vet.

Fact is, wir praying mantis
Is a prey to irrational fears,
And big Amanda
The panda
Husnae had it for years.

Aw bit, naw bit, yiv goat the wrang
Orangutang –
Aw bit, naw bit
Oor orangutang's got Angst.

Wir hyena's pure hysterical,
Wir chameleon's two faced
That big laugh
The lanky giraffe
Won't genuflect to the Human Race.

Aw bit, naw bit, yiv goat the wrang
Orangutang –
Aw bit, naw bit
Oor orangutang's goat Angst.

Oh they spike oor buns wi valium
And we swally 'em, we swally 'em.
Me an' the African Sociable Vulture
Urny happy in this alien culture –

Wir nocturnals are insomniac
And canny sleep till dark –
A' us animals are crackers,
Here in Calderpark.

Liz Lochhead

Do a Dance for Daddy

Do a dance for Daddy, make your Daddy smile
Be his little angel
Remember you're on trial
Mummy's competition, Mummy brings you down
When you're up there shining
She always wears a frown

Do a dance for Daddy. Bend and dip and whirl
You've got all that talent
'Cause you're Daddy's girl
Daddy is your hero, witty and superb
With a sign upon his door
That reads 'DO NOT DISTURB'

Look your best for Daddy
Pass your test for Daddy
Stand up tall for Daddy
Do it all for Daddy

Some day when you're older you will find romance
Someone just like Daddy
Will whistle and you'll dance
You'll recall that music when you're on the shelf
You danced for all the Daddies
But you never found yourself

Paint your eyes for Daddy
Win a prize for Daddy
Swim to France for Daddy
Do your dance for Daddy

Fran Landesman

Rotting Song

old green cheese
old green cheese
you'll never get another chance –

Green cheese sits in the airtight tin
wondering just how those mites got in,
crosses off the minutes to the sinking knife –
hasn't found out he's in prison for life

Cold meat sweats on the larder plate
a wet flesh target, doesn't have to wait,
in dive the black flies, drop their eggs –
drive him crazy those hairy legs

Dud plum squashed on the kitchen floor
can't see what he's been put there for,
knows he's going soft but he can't stir –
old age buries him deep in fur

Dud plum, cold meat, old green cheese
rot in your own time at your ease,
nobody minds, nobody cares –
moved out their lives and gone downstairs

Libby Houston

Not Waving But Drowning

Nobody heard him, the dead man,
But still he lay moaning:
I was much further out than you thought
And not waving but drowning.

Poor chap, he always loved larking
And now he's dead
It must have been too cold for him his heart gave way,
They said.

Oh, no no no, it was too cold always
(Still the dead one lay moaning)
I was much too far out all my life
And not waving but drowning.

Stevie Smith

Overheard in County Sligo

I married a man from County Roscommon
and I live at the back of beyond
with a field of cows and a yard of hens
and six white geese on the pond.

At my door's a square of yellow corn
caught up by its corners and shaken,
and the road runs down through the open gate
and freedom's there for the taking.

I had thought to work on the Abbey stage
or have my name in a book,
to see my thought on the printed page,
or still the crowd with a look.

But I turn to fold the breakfast cloth
and to polish the lustre and brass,
to order and dust the tumbled rooms
and find my face in the glass.

I ought to feel I'm a happy woman
for I lie in the lap of the land,
and I married a man from County Roscommon
and I live in the back of beyond.

Gillian Clarke

Egocentric

What care I if good God be
If he be not good to me,
If he will not hear my cry
Nor heed my melancholy midnight sigh?
What care I if he created Lamb,
And golden Lion, and mud-delighting Clam,
And Tiger stepping out on padded toe,
And the fecund earth the Blindworms know?
He made the Sun, the Moon and every Star,
He made the infant Owl and the Baboon,
He made the ruby-orbèd Pelican,
He made all silent inhumanity,
Nescient and quiescent to his will,
Unquickened by the questing conscious flame
That is my glory and my bitter bane.
What care I if Skies are blue,
If God created Gnat and Gnu,
What care I if good God be
If he be not good to me?

Stevie Smith

Happiness

Happiness is silent, or speaks equivocally for friends,
Grief is explicit and her song never ends,
Happiness is like England, and will not state a case,
Grief like Guilt rushes in and talks apace.

Stevie Smith

THE FLAT EARTH

A Lecture to the Flat Earth Society

As president of this worthy organization
And having been entrusted with the task
Of saving the poor souls who dwell too near
The Edge of the Earth from falling into
The Primal Dark beyond,
I would like to say:

My God I've lived all my life right here
On the Rim, the Brink, the Final Boundary of fear
With the long flat continents of dreams behind me
And nothing ahead but the sweet and terrible Night
I long to fall into, but do not dare.

What can I tell you, who inhabit with me
The Very Edge of the Abyss? We have no bathysphere
To explore the depths, no means whereby we can
    collect
The Abysmal Eggs of those creatures of the chasm
Who dwell in darkness below our heels.

As president of this worthy organization
I want to point out, without arousing any fear
That we are doomed on this Disc which spins its insane
    dreams
Through space. And those of us who always lived too
    near
The Edge to begin with

Have the consolation of each other's company,
The certain knowledge that the Night is also beautiful,
The abundant Night which spews out constantly before
    us
As the rays of a half-forgotten sun strike us from behind
On our delicate and unwinged heels.

Gwendolyn MacEwen

The Surgeon at 2 a.m.

The white light is artificial, and hygienic as heaven.
The microbes cannot survive it.
They are departing in their transparent garments,
   turned aside
From the scalpels and the rubber hands.
The scalded sheet is a snowfield, frozen and peaceful.
The body under it is in my hands.
As usual there is no face. A lump of Chinese white
With seven holes thumbed in. The soul is another light.
I have not seen it; it does not fly up.
Tonight it has receded like a ship's light.

It is a garden I have to do with – tubers and fruits
Oozing their jammy substances,
A mat of roots. My assistants hook them back.
Stenches and colours assail me.
This is the lung-tree.
These orchids are splendid. They spot and coil like
   snakes.
The heart is a red-bell-bloom, in distress.
I am so small
In comparison to these organs!
I worm and hack in a purple wilderness.

The blood is a sunset. I admire it.
I am up to my elbows in it, red and squeaking.
Still it seeps up, it is not exhausted.
So magical! A hot spring
I must seal off and let fill
The intricate, blue piping under this pale marble.

How I admire the Romans –
Aqueducts, the Baths of Caracalla, the eagle nose!
The body is a Roman thing.
It has shut its mouth on the stone pill of repose.

It is a statue the orderlies are wheeling off.
I have perfected it.
I am left with an arm or a leg,
A set of teeth, or stones
To rattle in a bottle and take home,
And tissue in slices – a pathological salami.
Tonight the parts are entombed in an icebox.
Tomorrow they will swim
In vinegar like saints' relics.
Tomorrow the patient will have a clean, pink plastic
    limb.

Over one bed in the ward, a small blue light
Announces a new soul. The bed is blue.
Tonight for this person, blue is a beautiful colour.
The angels of morphia have borne him up.
He floats an inch from the ceiling,
Smelling the dawn draughts.
I walk among sleepers in gauze sarcophagi.
The red night lights are flat moons. They are dull with
    blood.
I am the sun, in my white coat,
Grey faces, shuttered by drugs, follow me like flowers.

Sylvia Plath

Watching *Dark Circle*

'Why this is hell, nor am I out of it'
Marlowe, *Dr Faustus*

Men are willing to observe
the writhing, the bubbling flesh and
swift but protracted charring of bone
while the subject pigs, placed in cages designed for this,
don't pass out but continue to scream as they turn to
    cinder.
The Pentagon wants to know
something a child could tell it:
it hurts to burn, and even a match
can make you scream, pigs or people,
even the smallest common flame can kill you.
This plutonic calefaction is redundant.

Men are willing
to call the roasting of live pigs
a simulation of certain conditions. It is
not a simulation. The pigs (with their high-rated
    intelligence,
their uncanny precognition of disaster) are real,
their agony real agony, the smell
is not archetypal breakfast nor ancient feasting
but a foul miasma irremovable from the nostrils,
and the simulation of hell these men
have carefully set up
is hell itself,
             and they in it, dead in their lives,
and what can redeem them? What can redeem them?

Denise Levertov

Reading Hamlet

A dusty waste-plot by the cemetery,
Behind it, a river flasing blue.
You said to me: 'Go get thee to a nunnery,
Or get a fool to marry you . . . '

Well, princes are good at such speeches,
As a girl is quick to tears, –
But may those words stream like an ermine mantle
Behind him for ten thousand years.

Anna Akhmatova
translated by *D. M. Thomas*

Epilogue *from* Requiem

I

There I learned how faces fall apart,
How fear looks out from under the eyelids,
How deep are the hieroglyphics
Cut by suffering on people's cheeks.
There I learned how silver can inherit
The black, the ash-blond, overnight,
The smiles that faded from the poor in spirit,
Terror's dry coughing sound.
And I pray not only for myself,
But also for all those who stood there
In bitter cold, or in the July heat,
Under that red blind prison-wall.

II

Again the hands of the clock are nearing
The unforgettable hour. I see, hear, touch

All of you: the cripple they had to support
Painfully to the end of the line; the moribund;

And the girl who would shake her beautiful head and
Say: 'I come here as if it were home.'

I should like to call you all by name,
But they have lost the lists . . .

I have woven for them a great shroud
Out of the poor words I overheard them speak.

I remember them always and everywhere,
And if they shut my tormented mouth,

Through which a hundred million of my people cry,
Let them remember me also . . .

And if ever in this country they should want
To build me a monument

I consent to that honour,
But only on condition that they

Erect it not on the sea-shore where I was born:
My last links there were broken long ago,

Nor by the stump in the Royal Gardens,
Where an inconsolable young shade is seeking me,

But here, where I stood for three hundred hours
And where they never, never opened the doors for me.

Lest in blessed death I should forget
The grinding scream of the Black Marias,

The hideous clanging gate, the old
Woman wailing like a wounded beast.

And may the melting snow drop like tears
From my motionless bronze eyelids,

And the prison pigeons coo above me
And the ships sail slowly down the Neva.

Anna Akhmatova
translated by *D. M. Thomas*

Lot's Wife

And the just man trailed God's messenger,
His huge, light shape devoured the black hill.
But uneasiness shadowed his wife and spoke to her:
'It's not too late, you can look back still

At the red towers of Sodom, the place that bore you,
The square in which you sang, the spinning-shed,
At the empty windows of that upper storey
Where children blessed your happy marriage-bed.'

Her eyes that were still turning when a bolt
Of pain shot through them, were instantly blind;
Her body turned into transparent salt,
And her swift legs were rooted to the ground.

Who mourns one woman in a holocaust?
Surely her death has no significance?
Yet in my heart she never will be lost,
She who gave up her life to steal one glance.

Anna Akhmatova
translated by *D. M. Thomas*

The Woman Who Wanted to be a Hero

the first task was to persuade them
a woman could go
that my heart could and did ring
like warrior drums
that I could curtsey to dragons
and then slay them
that I could leap seven leagues
at the drop of a high-heeled boot
my mother and father complained
there was no farewell ritual for me
but I had brand-new disguises
and I needed to go

the second task was to search
in a dark wood for years
alone, and afraid, and not knowing
whether I touched
men, or gnarled trees, or hobgoblins
still, I learned songs, and the way of the wild
and the wise witch showed me
the way out of the wood

the third and hardest task
is letting you search for me
through thorns, over glass-topped walls
past siren music
and the sleepy drugs of flowers
I must stand still, I must wait
wet, humming aloud, smelling
sweet, smelling strong

74

certainly, I have few words
and no tricks
for this

Michèle Roberts

Poem on the Day of the
Autumn Equinox

she's going, the nice girl who smiled
all the time
crossing her legs
her fingertips dipping
at sugar–
bowls and at skinny bread

leaving home, the warm
family smell and the games with mum
– the sky tears in two, grey cartridge paper

on the street
vulnerability lures
like the tang of blood, a single
flick of the razorblade
– of course, she murmurs, of course
I can see that

the new flat, uncurtained, floats
high up and lit; it's
no halo of steel; when she closes her eyes
the noises pad into her bed: such impudence!
on the floor above, a woman
screams rhythmically, and she cannot stop it
nor her lover's curses; their duet is terrible
below: shouts, and shattering glass
a brick? a bottle? in whose face?
next door, a soft shuffle: the avuncular
slippers of torturers

she lies down alone; independence
flickers off–
on, a worn neon sign; she watches the blue
night, bunched like policemen
muscle in through the window; she faces
the dark
beginning again

Michèle Roberts

Baby-Sitting

I am sitting in a strange room listening
For the wrong baby. I don't love
This baby. She is sleeping a snuffly
Roseate, bubbling sleep; she is fair;
She is a perfectly acceptable child.
I am afraid of her. If she wakes
She will hate me. She will shout
Her hot midnight rage, her nose
Will stream disgustingly and the perfume
Of her breath will fail to enchant me.

To her I will represent absolute
Abandonment. For her it will be worse
Than for the lover cold in lonely
Sheets; worse than for the woman who waits
A moment to collect her dignity
Beside the bleached bone in the terminal ward.
As she rises sobbing from the monstrous land
Stretching for milk-familiar comforting,
She will find me and between us two
It will not come. It will not come.

Gillian Clarke

The Woman Who Could Not Live
with Her Faulty Heart

I do not mean the symbol
of love, a candy shape
to decorate cakes with,
the heart that is supposed
to belong or break;

I mean this lump of muscle
that contracts like a flayed biceps,
purple-blue, with its skin of suet,
its skin of gristle, this isolate,
this caved hermit, unshelled
turtle, this one lungful of blood,
no happy plateful.

All hearts float in their own
deep oceans of no light,
wetblack and glimmering,
their four mouths gulping like fish.
Hearts are said to pound:
this is to be expected, the heart's
regular struggle against being drowned.

But most hearts say, I want, I want,
I want, I want. My heart
is more duplicitous,
though no twin as I once thought.
It says, I want, I don't want, I
want, and then a pause.
It forces me to listen,

and at night it is the infra-red
third eye that remains open
while the other two are sleeping
but refuses to say what it has seen.

It is a constant pestering
in my ears, a caught moth, limping drum,
a child's fist beating
itself against the bedsprings:
I want, I don't want.
How can one live with such a heart?

Long ago I gave up singing
to it, it will never be satisfied or lulled.
One night I will say to it:
Heart, be still,
and it will.

Margaret Atwood

Some People's Dreams Pay All Their Bills

Some people's dreams pay all their bills,
While others' gild an empty shell ...
But mine go whimpering about a velvet dress,
Cherry-red and sumptuous as sin.
O, inaccessible! Not of our world!
Nowhere to get you, or to put you on ...
But how I want you!
Against all reason's reproaches –
There, in the very narrows of the heart's
Recesses – flourishes the poison
Of heavy folds, and obscure embroidery ...
The childish, flouted right
To beauty! Not bread, not domicile –
But unbleached, royal lace,
Enspiralled rings, sly ribbons – but no!
My day is like a donkey, bridled, laden,
My night deserted, like the prison light.
But in my soul – it's no good! I am guilty! –
I keep on sewing it, and in my mind I make
The thousandth stitch, as I do up my anorak
And try on my tarpaulin boots.

Irina Ratushinskaya
translated by *David McDuff*

About Death

And at the moment of death
what is correct procedure?

Cut the umbilicus, they said.

And with the umbilicus cut
how then prepare the body?

Wash it in sacred water.
Dress it in silk for the wedding.

P. K. Page

Part Two
Eminent Victorians

ELIZABETH BARRETT BROWNING 1806–1861

CHRISTINA ROSSETTI 1830–1894

EMILY DICKINSON 1830–1886

ELIZABETH BARRETT BROWNING

The following piece is extracted from a major epic
poem 'Aurora Leigh', first published in 1856 when
Elizabeth Barrett Browning was at the height of her
power and fame. It is primarily a political poem, with a
strong narrative that makes it compelling reading. In
this extract the heroine Aurora (a young poet) is
proposed to by her rich cousin Romney Leigh.

In the passage preceding this extract, Romney
surprises Aurora in the middle of a private ceremony
where she has just crowned herself with a laurel of ivy,
in acknowledgement of her own achievement as a poet.
Boasting that he hasn't read a page of her poetry,
Romney assures Aurora that her talent as a poet is of no
account, as women cannot write great poetry, and
advises her that her energies would be better spent in
doing nobler work. He tells her how full of vice and
suffering the world is, and how he intends to devote his
life to improving it if he can.

Aurora acknowledges the nobility of his intentions
and ends by saying (not without irony), 'Accept my
reverence'.

Romney's Proposal
from Aurora Leigh

          There he glowed on me
With all his face and eyes. 'No other help?'
Said he – 'no more than so?'
                     'What help?' I asked.
'You'd scorn my help, – as Nature's self, you say,
Has scorned to put her music in my mouth
Because a woman's. Do you now turn round
And ask for what a woman cannot give?'

'For what she only can, I turn and ask,'
He answered, catching up my hands in his,
And dropping on me from his high-eaved brow
The full weight of his soul, – 'I ask for love,
And that, she can; for life in fellowship
Through bitter duties – that, I know she can;
For wifehood – will she?'
                  'Now,' I said, 'may God
Be witness 'twixt us two!' and with the word,
Meseemed I floated into a sudden light
Above his stature, – 'am I proved too weak
To stand alone, yet strong enough to bear
Such leaners on my shoulder? poor to think,
Yet rich enough to sympathise with thought?
Incompetent to sing, as blackbirds can,
Yet competent to love, like HIM?'
                      I paused;
Perhaps I darkened, as the lighthouse will
That turns upon the sea. 'It's always so.
Anything does for a wife.'
                  'Aurora, dear,
And dearly honoured,' – he pressed in at once
With eager utterance, – 'you translate me ill.
I do not contradict my thought of you

Which is most reverent, with another thought
Found less so. If your sex is weak for art
(And I, who said so, did but honour you
By using truth in courtship), it is strong
For life and duty. Place your fecund heart
In mine, and let us blossom for the world
That wants love's colour in the grey of time.
My talk, meanwhile, is arid to you, ay,
Since all my talk can only set you where
You look down coldly on the arena-heaps
Of headless bodies, shapeless, indistinct!
The Judgment-Angel scarce would find his way
Through such a heap of generalised distress
To the individual man with lips and eyes,
Much less Aurora. Ah, my sweet, come down,
And hand in hand we'll go where yours shall touch
These victims, one by one! till, one by one,
The formless, nameless trunk of every man
Shall seem to wear a head with hair you know,
And every woman catch your mother's face
To melt you into passion.'

                            'I am a girl,'
I answered slowly; 'you do well to name
My mother's face. Though far too early, alas,
God's hand did interpose 'twixt it and me,
I know so much of love as used to shine
In that face and another. Just so much;
No more indeed at all. I have not seen
So much love since, I pray you pardon me,
As answers even to make a marriage with
In this cold land of England. What you love
Is not a woman, Romney, but a cause:
You want a helpmate, not a mistress, sir,
A wife to help your ends, – in her no end.
Your cause is noble, your ends excellent,
But I being most unworthy of these and that,
Do otherwise conceive of love. Farewell.'

88

'Farewell, Aurora? you reject me thus?'
He said.
            'Sir, you were married long ago.
You have a wife already whom you love,
Your social theory. Bless you both, I say.
For my part, I am scarcely meek enough
To be the handmaid of a lawful spouse.
Do I look a Hagar, think you?'
                              'So you jest.'

'Nay, so, I speak in earnest,' I replied.
'You treat of marriage too much like, at least,
A chief apostle: you would bear with you
A wife . . . a sister . . . shall we speak it out?
A sister of charity.'
                    'Then, must it be
Indeed farewell? And was I so far wrong
In hope and in illusion, when I took
The woman to be nobler than the man,
Yourself the noblest woman, in the use
And comprehension of what love is, – love,
That generates the likeness of itself
Through all heroic duties? so far wrong,
In saying bluntly, venturing truth on love,
"Come, human creature, love and work with me," –
Instead of "Lady, thou art wondrous fair,
And, where the Graces walk before, the Muse
Will follow at the lightning of their eyes,
And where the Muse walks, lovers need to creep:
Turn round and love me, or I die of love."' '

With quiet indignation I broke in.
'You misconceive the question like a man,
Who sees a woman as the complement
Of his sex merely. You forget too much
That every creature, female as the male,

Stands single in responsible act and thought
As also in birth and death. Whoever says
To a loyal woman, "Love and work with me,"
Will get fair answers if the work and love,
Being good themselves, are good for her – the best
She was born for. Women of a softer mood,
Surprised by men when scarcely awake to life,
Will sometimes only hear the first word, love,
And catch up with it any kind of work,
Indifferent, so that dear love go with it.
I do not blame such women, though, for love,
They pick much oakum; earth's fanatics make
Too frequently heaven's saints. But *me* your work
Is not the best for, – nor your love the best,
Nor able to commend the kind of work
For love's sake merely. Ah, you force me, sir,
To be overbold in speaking of myself:
I too have my vocation, – work to do,
The heavens and earth have set me since I changed
My father's face for theirs, and, though your world
Were twice as wretched as you represent,
Most serious work, most necessary work
As any of the economists'. Reform,
Make trade a Christian possibility,
And individual right no general wrong;
Wipe out earth's furrows of the Thine and Mine,
And leave one green for men to play at bowls,
With innings for them all! . . . What then, indeed,
If mortals are not greater by the head
Than any of their prosperities? what then,
Unless the artist keep up open roads
Betwixt the seen and unseen, – bursting through
The best of your conventions with his best,
The speakable, imaginable best
God bids him speak, to prove what lies beyond
Both speech and imagination? A starved man

Exceeds a fat beast: we'll not barter, sir,
The beautiful for barley. – And, even so,
I hold you will not compass your poor ends
Of barley-feeding and material ease,
Without a poet's individualism
To work your universal. It takes a soul,
To move a body: it takes a high-souled man,
To move the masses, even to a cleaner stye:
It takes the ideal, to blow a hair's breadth off
The dust of the actual. – Ah, your Fouriers failed,
Because not poets enough to understand
That life develops from within. – For me,
Perhaps I am not worthy, as you say,
Of work like this: perhaps a woman's soul
Aspires, and not creates: yet we aspire,
And yet I'll try out your perhapses, sir,
And if I fail . . . why, burn me up my straw
Like other false works – I'll not ask for grace;
Your scorn is better, cousin Romney. I
Who love my art, would never wish it lower
To suit my stature. I may love my art.
You'll grant that even a woman may love art,
Seeing that to waste true love on anything
Is womanly, past question.'
                                         I retain
The very last word which I said that day,
As you the creaking of the door, years past,
Which let upon you such disabling news
You ever after have been graver. He,
His eyes, the motions in his silent mouth,
Were fiery points on which my words were caught,
Transfixed for ever in my memory
For his sake, not their own. And yet I know
I did not love him . . . nor he me . . . that's sure . . .
And what I said is unrepented of,

As truth is always. Yet . . . a princely man! –
If hard to me, heroic for himself!
He bears down on me through the slanting years,
The stronger for the distance. If he had loved,
Ay, loved me, with that retributive face, . . .
I might have been a common woman now
And happier, less known and less left alone,
Perhaps a better woman after all,
With chubby children hanging on my neck
To keep me low and wise. Ah me, the vines
That bear such fruit are proud to stoop with it.
The palm stands upright in a realm of sand.
And I, who spoke the truth then, stand upright,
Still worthy of having spoken out the truth,
By being content I spoke it though it set
Him there, me here. – O woman's vile remorse,
To hanker after a mere name, a show;
A supposition, a potential love!
Does every man who names love in our lives
Become a power for that? is love's true thing
So much best to us, that what personates love
Is next best? A potential love, forsooth!
I'm not so vile. No, no – he cleaves, I think,
This man, this image, – chiefly for the wrong
And shock he gave my life, in finding me
Precisely where the devil of my youth
Had set me, on those mountain-peaks of hope
All glittering with the dawn-dew, all erect
And famished for the noon, – exclaiming, while
I looked for empire and much tribute, 'Come,
I have some worthy work for thee below.
Come, sweep my barns and keep my hospitals,
And I will pay thee with a current coin
Which men give women.'
                              As we spoke, the grass
Was trod in haste beside us, and my aunt,

With smile distorted by the sun, – face, voice
As much at issue with the summer-day
As if you brought a candle out of doors,
Broke in with 'Romney, here! – My child, entreat
Your cousin to the house, and have your talk,
If girls must talk upon their birthdays. Come.'

He answered for me calmly, with pale lips
That seemed to motion for a smile in vain,
'The talk is ended, madam, where we stand.
Your brother's daughter has dismissed me here;
And all my answer can be better said
Beneath the trees, than wrong by such a word
Your house's hospitalities. Farewell.'

With that he vanished. I could hear his heel
Ring bluntly in the lane, as down he leapt
The short way from us. – Then a measured speech
Withdrew me. 'What means this, Aurora Leigh?
My brother's daughter has dismissed my guests?'

The lion in me felt the keeper's voice
Through all its quivering dewlaps; I was quelled
Before her, – meekened to the child she knew:
I prayed her pardon, said 'I had little thought
To give dismissal to a guest of hers,
In letting go a friend of mine who came
To take me into service as a wife, –
No more than that, indeed.'

                              'No more, no more?
Pray Heaven,' she answered, 'that I was not mad.
I could not mean to tell her to her face
That Romney Leigh had asked me for a wife,
And I refused him?'

                              'Did he ask?' I said;
'I think he rather stooped to take me up

For certain uses which he found to do
For something called a wife. He never asked.'

'What stuff!' she answered; 'are they queens, these girls?
They must have mantles, stitched with twenty silks,
Spread out upon the ground, before they'll step
One footstep for the noblest lover born.'

'But I am born,' I said with firmness, 'I,
To walk another way than his, dear aunt.'

Elizabeth Barrett Browning

CHRISTINA ROSSETTI

'Goblin Market' is the title poem of Christina Rossetti's first book of poems, published when she was thirty-one. Critics describe it as 'elusive', 'deeply perverse', 'enigmatic' but the sensuousness of the poem is undisputed. However one may choose to interpret the undertext, the poem emerges as a celebration of love between women, and a dire warning against 'Goblin Fruit'. At the time when 'Goblin Market' was being written, Rossetti's brother, with whom she was very close, was involved in a passionate but destructive relationship with Lizzie Siddal, who subsequently took her own life. Christina Rossetti never married. It is said that she turned down two proposals of marriage, and among her later poems are a number of love poems addressed to women.

Goblin Market

Morning and evening
Maids heard the goblins cry:
'Come buy our orchard fruits,
Come buy, come buy:
Apples and quinces,
Lemons and oranges,
Plump unpecked cherries,
Melons and raspberries,
Bloom-down-cheeked peaches,
Swart-headed mulberries,
Wild free-born cranberries,
Crab-apples, dewberries,
Pine-apples, blackberries,
Apricots, strawberries; –
All ripe together
In summer weather, –
Morns that pass by,
Fair eves that fly;
Come buy, come buy:
Our grapes fresh from the vine,
Pomegranates full and fine,
Dates and sharp bullaces,
Rare pears and greengages,
Damsons and bilberries,
Taste them and try:
Currants and gooseberries,
Bright-fire-like barberries,
Figs to fill your mouth,
Citrons from the South,
Sweet to tongue and sound to eye;
Come buy, come buy.'

Evening by evening
Among the brookside rushes,
Laura bowed her head to hear,
Lizzie veiled her blushes:
Crouching close together
In the cooling weather,
With clasping arms and cautioning lips,
With tingling cheeks and finger tips.
'Lie close,' Laura said,
Pricking up her golden head:
'We must not look at goblin men,
We must not buy their fruits:
Who knows upon what soil they fed
Their hungry thirsty roots?'
'Come buy,' call the goblins
Hobbling down the glen.
'Oh,' cried Lizzie, 'Laura, Laura,
You should not peep at goblin men.'
Lizzie covered up her eyes,
Covered close lest they should look;
Laura reared her glossy head,
And whispered like the restless brook:
'Look, Lizzie, look, Lizzie,
Down the glen tramp little men.
One hauls a basket,
One bears a plate,
One lugs a golden dish
Of many pounds weight.
How fair the vine must grow
Whose grapes are so luscious;
How warm the wind must blow
Through those fruit bushes.'
'No,' said Lizzie: 'No, no, no;
Their offers should not charm us,
Their evil gifts would harm us.'
She thrust a dimpled finger

In each ear, shut eyes and ran:
Curious Laura chose to linger
Wondering at each merchant man.
One had a cat's face,
One whisked a tail,
One tramped at a rat's pace,
One crawled like a snail,
One like a wombat prowled obtuse and furry,
One like a ratel tumbled hurry skurry.
She heard a voice like voice of doves
Cooing all together:
They sounded kind and full of loves
In the pleasant weather.

    Laura stretched her gleaming neck
Like a rush-imbedded swan,
Like a lily from the beck,
Like a moonlit poplar branch,
Like a vessel at the launch
When its last restraint is gone.

    Backwards up the mossy glen
Turned and trooped the goblin men,
With their shrill repeated cry,
'Come buy, come buy.'
When they reached where Laura was
They stood stock still upon the moss,
Leering at each other,
Brother with queer brother;
Signalling each other,
Brother with sly brother.
One set his basket down,
One reared his plate;
One began to weave a crown
Of tendrils, leaves, and rough nuts brown
(Men sell not such in any town);

One heaved the golden weight
Of dish and fruit to offer her:
'Come buy, come buy,' was still their cry.
Laura stared but did not stir,
Longed but had no money:
The whisk-tailed merchant bade her taste
In tones as smooth as honey,
The cat-faced purr'd,
The rat-paced spoke a word
Of welcome, and the snail-paced even was heard;
One parrot-voiced and jolly
Cried 'Pretty Goblin' still for 'Pretty Polly;' –
One whistled like a bird.

But sweet-tooth Laura spoke in haste:
'Good folk, I have no coin;
To take were to purloin:
I have no copper in my purse,
I have no silver either,
And all my gold is on the furze
That shakes in windy weather
Above the rusty heather.'
'You have much gold upon your head,'
They answered all together:
'Buy from us with a golden curl.'
She clipped a precious golden lock,
She dropped a tear more rare than pearl,
Then sucked their fruit globes fair or red:
Sweeter than honey from the rock,
Stronger than man-rejoicing wine,
Clearer than water flowed that juice;
She never tasted such before,
How should it cloy with length of use?
She sucked and sucked and sucked the more
Fruits which that unknown orchard bore;
She sucked until her lips were sore;

Then flung the emptied rinds away
But gathered up one kernel stone,
And knew not was it night or day
As she turned home alone.
  Lizzie met her at the gate
Full of wise upbraidings:
'Dear, you should not stay so late,
Twilight is not good for maidens;
Should not loiter in the glen
In the haunts of goblin men.
Do you not remember Jeanie,
How she met them in the moonlight,
Took their gifts both choice and many,
Ate their fruits and wore their flowers
Plucked from bowers
Where summer ripens at all hours?
But ever in the noonlight
She pined and pined away;
Sought them by night and day,
Found them no more but dwindled and grew grey;
Then fell with the first snow,
While to this day no grass will grow
Where she lies low:
I planted daisies there a year ago
That never blow.
You should not loiter so.'
'Nay, hush,' said Laura:
'Nay, hush, my sister:
I ate and ate my fill,
Yet my mouth waters still;
To-morrow night I will
Buy more:' and kissed her:
'Have done with sorrow;
I'll bring you plums to-morrow
Fresh on their mother twigs,
Cherries worth getting;

You cannot think what figs
My teeth have met in,
What melons icy-cold
Piled on a dish of gold
Too huge for me to hold,
What peaches with a velvet nap,
Pellucid grapes without one seed:
Odorous indeed must be the mead
Whereon they grow, and pure the wave they drink
With lilies at the brink,
And sugar-sweet their sap.'

Golden head by golden head,
Like two pigeons in one nest
Folded in each other's wings,
They lay down in their curtained bed:
Like two blossoms on one stem,
Like two flakes of new-fall'n snow,
Like two wands of ivory
Tipped with gold for awful kings.
Moon and stars gazed in at them,
Wind sang to them lullaby,
Lumbering owls forbore to fly,
Not a bat flapped to and fro
Round their nest:
Cheek to cheek and breast to breast
Locked together in one nest.

Early in the morning
When the first cock crowed his warning,
Neat like bees, as sweet and busy,
Laura rose with Lizzie:
Fetched in honey, milked the cows,
Aired and set to rights the house,
Kneaded cakes of whitest wheat,
Cake for dainty mouths to eat,
Next churned butter, whipped up cream,

Fed their poultry, sat and sewed;
Talked as modest maidens should:
Lizzie with an open heart,
Laura in an absent dream,
One content, one sick in part;
One warbling for the mere bright day's delight,
One longing for the night.

At length slow evening came:
They went with pitchers to the reedy brook;
Lizzie most placid in her look,
Laura most like a leaping flame.
They drew the gurgling water from its deep;
Lizzie plucked purple and rich golden flags,
Then turning homewards said: 'The sunset flushes
Those furthest loftiest crags;
Come, Laura, not another maiden lags,
No wilful squirrel wags,
The beasts and birds are fast asleep.'
But Laura loitered still among the rushes
And said the bank was steep.

And said the hour was early still,
The dew not fall'n, the wind not chill:
Listening ever, but not catching
The customary cry,
'Come buy, come buy,'
With its iterated jingle
Of sugar-baited words:
Not for all her watching
Once discerning even one goblin
Racing, whisking, tumbling, hobbling;
Let alone the herds
That used to tramp along the glen,
In groups or single,
Of brisk fruit-merchant men.

Till Lizzie urged, 'O Laura, come;
I hear the fruit-call but I dare not look:
You should not loiter longer at this brook:
Come with me home.
The stars rise, the moon bends her arc,
Each glowworm winks her spark,
Let us get home before the night grows dark:
For clouds may gather
Though this is summer weather,
Put out the lights and drench us through;
Then if we lost our way what should we do?'

    Laura turned cold as stone
To find her sister heard that cry alone,
That goblin cry,
'Come buy our fruits, come buy.'
Must she then buy no more such dainty fruit?
Must she no more such succous pasture find,
Gone deaf and blind?
Her tree of life drooped from the root:
She said not one word in her heart's sore ache;
But peering thro' the dimness, nought discerning,
Trudged home, her pitcher dripping all the way;
So crept to bed, and lay
Silent till Lizzie slept;
Then sat up in a passionate yearning,
And gnashed her teeth for baulked desire, and wept
As if her heart would break.

    Day after day, night after night,
Laura kept watch in vain
In sullen silence of exceeding pain.
She never caught again the goblin cry:
'Come buy, come buy;' –
She never spied the goblin men
Hawking their fruits along the glen:

But when the noon waxed bright
Her hair grew thin and grey;
She dwindled, as the fair full moon doth turn
To swift decay and burn
Her fire away.

One day remembering her kernel-stone
She set it by a wall that faced the south;
Dewed it with tears, hoped for a root,
Watched for a waxing shoot,
But there came none;
It never saw the sun,
It never felt the trickling moisture run:
While with sunk eyes and faded mouth
She dreamed of melons, as a traveller sees
False waves in desert drouth
With shade of leaf-crowned trees,
And burns the thirstier in the sandful breeze.

She no more swept the house,
Tended the fowls or cows,
Fetched honey, kneaded cakes of wheat,
Brought water from the brook:
But sat down listless in the chimney-nook
And would not eat.

Tender Lizzie could not bear
To watch her sister's cankerous care
Yet not to share.
She night and morning
Caught the goblins' cry:
'Come buy our orchard fruits,
Come buy, come buy:' –
Beside the brook, along the glen,
She heard the tramp of goblin men,
The voice and stir

Poor Laura could not hear;
Longed to buy fruit to comfort her,
But feared to pay too dear.
She thought of Jeanie in her grave,
Who should have been a bride;
But who for joys brides hope to have
Fell sick and died
In her gay prime,
In earliest Winter time,
With the first glazing rime,
With the first snow-fall of crisp Winter time.

   Till Laura dwindling
Seemed knocking at Death's door:
Then Lizzie weighed no more
Better and worse;
But put a silver penny in her purse,
Kissed Laura, crossed the heath with

                  clumps of furze

At twilight, halted by the brook:
And for the first time in her life
Began to listen and look.

   Laughed every goblin
When they spied her peeping:
Came towards her hobbling,
Flying, running, leaping,
Puffing and blowing,
Chuckling, clapping, crowing,
Clucking and gobbling,
Mopping and mowing,
Full of airs and graces,
Pulling wry faces,
Demure grimaces,
Cat-like and rat-like,
Ratel- and wombat-like,

Snail-paced in a hurry,
Parrot-voiced and whistler,
Helter skelter, hurry skurry,
Chattering like magpies,
Fluttering like pigeons,
Gliding like fishes, –
Hugged her and kissed her:
Squeezed and caressed her:
Stretched up their dishes,
Panniers, and plates:
'Look at our apples
Russet and dun,
Bob at our cherries,
Bite at our peaches,
Citrons and dates,
Grapes for the asking,
Pears red with basking
Out in the sun,
Plums on their twigs;
Pluck them and suck them,
Pomegranates, figs.' –

'Good folk,' said Lizzie,
Mindful of Jeanie:
'Give me much and many:' –
Held out her apron,
Tossed them her penny.
'Nay, take a seat with us,
Honour and eat with us,'
They answered grinning:
'Our feast is but beginning.
Night yet is early,
Warm and dew-pearly,
Wakeful and starry:
Such fruits as these
No man can carry;

Half their bloom would fly,
Half their dew would dry,
Half their flavour would pass by.
Sit down and feast with us,
Be welcome guest with us,
Cheer you and rest with us.' –
'Thank you,' said Lizzie: 'But one waits
At home alone for me:
So without further parleying,
If you will not sell me any
Of your fruits though much and many,
Give me back my silver penny
I tossed you for a fee.' –
They began to scratch their pates,
No longer wagging, purring,
But visibly demurring,
Grunting and snarling.
One called her proud,
Cross-grained, uncivil;
Their tones waxed loud,
Their looks were evil.
Lashing their tails
They trod and hustled her,
Elbowed and jostled her,
Clawed with their nails,
Barking, mewing, hissing, mocking,
Tore her gown and soiled her stocking,
Twitched her hair out by the roots,
Stamped upon her tender feet,
Held her hands and squeezed their fruits
Against her mouth to make her eat.

    White and golden Lizzie stood,
Like a lily in a flood, –
Like a rock of blue-veined stone
Lashed by tides obstreperously, –

Like a beacon left alone
In a hoary roaring sea,
Sending up a golden fire, –
Like a fruit-crowned orange-tree
White with blossoms honey-sweet
Sore beset by wasp and bee, –
Like a royal virgin town
Topped with gilded dome and spire
Close beleaguered by a fleet
Mad to tug her standard down.

    One may lead a horse to water,
Twenty cannot make him drink.
Though the goblins cuffed and caught her,
Coaxed and fought her,
Bullied and besought her,
Scratched her, pinched her black as ink,
Kicked and knocked her,
Mauled and mocked her,
Lizzie uttered not a word;
Would not open lip from lip
Lest they should cram a mouthful in:
But laughed in heart to feel the drip
Of juice that syrupped all her face,
And lodged in dimples of her chin,
And streaked her neck which quaked like curd.
At last the evil people
Worn out by her resistance
Flung back her penny, kicked their fruit
Along whichever road they took,
Not leaving root or stone or shoot;
Some writhed into the ground,
Some dived into the brook
With ring and ripple,
Some scudded on the gale without a sound,
Some vanished in the distance.

In a smart, ache, tingle,
Lizzie went her way;
Knew not was it night or day;
Sprang up the bank, tore thro' the furze,
Threaded copse and dingle,
And heard her penny jingle
Bouncing in her purse, –
Its bounce was music to her ear.
She ran and ran
As if she feared some goblin man
Dogged her with gibe or curse
Or something worse:
But not one goblin skurried after,
Nor was she pricked by fear;
The kind heart made her windy-paced
That urged her home quite out of breath with haste
And inward laughter.

She cried 'Laura,' up the garden,
'Did you miss me?
Come and kiss me.
Never mind my bruises,
Hug me, kiss me, suck my juices
Squeezed from goblin fruits for you,
Goblin pulp and goblin dew.
Eat me, drink me, love me;
Laura, make much of me:
For your sake I have braved the glen
And had to do with goblin merchant men.'

Laura started from her chair,
Flung her arms up in the air,
Clutched her hair:
'Lizzie, Lizzie, have you tasted
For my sake the fruit forbidden?
Must your light like mine be hidden,

Your young life like mine be wasted,
Undone in mine undoing
And ruined in my ruin,
Thirsty, cankered, goblin-ridden?' –
She clung about her sister,
Kissed and kissed and kissed her:
Tears once again
Refreshed her shrunken eyes,
Dropping like rain
After long sultry drouth;
Shaking with anguish, fear, and pain,
She kissed and kissed her with a hungry mouth.

   Her lips began to scorch,
That juice was wormwood to her tongue,
She loathed the feast:
Writhing as one possessed she leaped and sung,
Rent all her robe, and wrung
Her hands in lamentable haste,
And beat her breast.
Her locks streamed like the torch
Borne by a racer at full speed,
Or like the mane of horses in their flight,
Or like an eagle when she stems the light
Straight toward the sun,
Or like a caged thing freed,
Or like a flying flag when armies run.

   Swift fire spread through her veins, knocked at
     her heart,
Met the fire smouldering there
And overbore its lesser flame;
She gorged on bitterness without a name:
Ah! fool, to choose such part
Of soul-consuming care!
Sense failed in the mortal strife:

Like the watch-tower of a town
Which an earthquake shatters down,
Like a lightning-stricken mast,
Like a wind-uprooted tree
Spun about,
Like a foam-topped waterspout
Cast down headlong in the sea,
She fell at last;
Pleasure past and anguish past,
Is it death or is it life?

　　Life out of death.
That night long Lizzie watched by her,
Counted her pulse's flagging stir,
Felt for her breath,
Held water to her lips, and cooled her face
With tears and fanning leaves:
But when the first birds chirped about their eaves,
And early reapers plodded to the place
Of golden sheaves,
And dew-wet grass
Bowed in the morning winds so brisk to pass,
And new buds with new day
Opened of cup-like lilies on the stream,
Laura awoke as from a dream,
Laughed in the innocent old way,
Hugged Lizzie but not twice or thrice;
Her gleaming locks showed not one thread of grey,
Her breath was sweet as May
And light danced in her eyes.

　　Days, weeks, months, years
Afterwards, when both were wives
With children of their own;
Their mother-hearts beset with fears,
Their lives bound up in tender lives;

Laura would call the little ones
And tell them of her early prime,
Those pleasant days long gone
Of not-returning time:
Would talk about the haunted glen,
The wicked, quaint fruit-merchant men,
Their fruits like honey to the throat
But poison in the blood;
(Men sell not such in any town:)
Would tell them how her sister stood
In deadly peril to do her good,
And win the fiery antidote:
Then joining hands to little hands
Would bid them cling together,
'For there is no friend like a sister
In calm or stormy weather;
To cheer one on the tedious way,
To fetch one if one goes astray,
To lift one if one totters down,
To strengthen whilst one stands.'

Christina Rossetti

EMILY DICKINSON

Emily Dickinson was born in Amhurst, Massachusetts, where she lived in almost complete seclusion from all but her immediate family and a few close friends. She wrote a total of one thousand seven hundred and seventy five poems, only seven of which were published during her lifetime. After her death in 1886, her sister found her poems bound together in little booklets in a chest in her bedroom. The discovery of a mass of unpublished, unsuspected poetry by one of the greatest poets of the English language was perhaps one of the great dramas of literary history.

Dickinson's seclusion from the world did not mean that she was ignorant of other writers and the literary world around her. But rather than try to conform to the literary tastes of the time, she chose to pursue her own genius with extraordinary conviction and commitment. Her subject was inner exploration, and in the single room where she spent most of her time in isolation, she lived a life charged with intensity and vision.

Early editors of her work tried to improve on it by making it less 'eccentric' and released the poems gradually between 1890 and 1945. It was not until 1955 that the complete body of her work was published as she had originally written it. The five poems included here are in their original form, with the dates of their first publication.

First published 1929

I took one Draught of Life –
I'll tell you what I paid –
Precisely an existence –
The market price, they said.

They weighed me, Dust by Dust –
They balanced Film with Film,
Then handed me my Being's worth –
A single Dram of Heaven!

First published 1866

A narrow Fellow in the Grass
Occasionally rides –
You may have met Him – did you not
His notice sudden is –

The Grass divides as with a Comb –
A spotted shaft is seen –
And then it closes at your feet
And opens further on –

He likes a Boggy Acre
A Floor too cool for Corn –
Yet when a Boy, and Barefoot –
I more than once at Noon

Have passed, I thought, a Whip lash
Unbraiding in the Sun
When stooping to secure it
It wrinkled, and was gone –

Several of Nature's People
I know, and they know me –
I feel for them a transport
Of cordiality –

But never met this Fellow
Attended, or alone
Without a tighter breathing
And Zero at the Bone –

First published 1945

The Loneliness One dare not sound –
And would as soon surmise
As in its Grave go plumbing
To ascertain the size –

The Loneliness whose worst alarm
Is lest itself should see –
And perish from before itself
For just a scrutiny –

The Horror not to be surveyed –
But skirted in the Dark –
With Consciousness suspended –
And Being under Lock –

I fear me this – is Loneliness –
The Maker of the soul
Its Caverns and its Corridors
Illuminate – or seal –

First published 1914

That Love is all there is,
Is all we know of Love;
It is enough, the freight should be
Proportioned to the groove.

First published 1890

The Soul selects her own Society –
Then – shuts the Door –
To her divine Majority –
Present no more –

Unmoved – she notes the Chariots – pausing –
At her low Gate –
Unmoved – an Emperor be kneeling
Upon her Mat –

I've known her – from an ample nation –
Choose One –
Then – close the Valves of her attention –
Like Stone –

Emily Dickinson

Part Three
Two Poems from Oral Traditions

THE CHARM OF THE CHURN
Recited by Mary MacLeillan

THE STORY OF NANGSA OBUM
Told by Tsultrim Allione

THE CHARM OF THE CHURN (Hebrides)

Recited by Mary MacLeillan between 1855–1899,
recorded, and translated from the Gaelic by Alexander
Carmichael.

There was a time when poems were spoken and sung in
the highlands of Scotland as a part of the normal,
everyday life of the people. There were poems to work
to, poems to cure the sick, poems to make the cow
produce milk, or the lost one come home. They were
never written down, but passed on, from mother to
daughter and father to son, down the generations. They
contained the collective wisdom, history, medical
knowledge, and spiritual power of a great people – as
well as their fairy tales and superstitions and gossip.

   The spell included here, 'The Charm of the Churn',
was spoken by the women as they churned cream by
hand, to make it turn into butter – a long job that
needed a lot of staying power to get it done, and some
magic too. Malevolent energies could hamper the work.
The ill-wish of a neighbour, for example, could prevent
the coming of butter in the churn. Here the reciter
invokes the powers of her Christian faith, as well as the
powers of nature, to help her in her task. She invites all
creatures, blessed and unblessed, to metaphorically
drink from her churn to reduce the liquid.

The Charm of the Churn

Come will the free, come;
Come will the bond, come;
Come will the bells, come;
Come will the maers, come;
Come will the blade, come;
Come will the sharp, come;
Come will the hounds, come;
Come will the wild, come;
Come will the mild, come;
Come will the kind, come;
Come will the loving, come;
Come will the squint, come;
Come will he of the yellow cap,
That will set the churn a-running.

The free will come,
The bond will come,
The bells will come,
The maers will come,
The blades will come,
The sharp will come,
The hounds will come,
The wild will come,
The mild will come,
The kind will come,
The loving will come,
The devious will come,
The brim-full of the glove will come,
To set the churn a-running;
The kindly Columba will come in his array,
And the golden-haired Bride of the kine.

A splash is here,
A plash is here,
A plash is here,
A splash is here,
A crash is here,
A squash is here,
A squash is here,
A crash is here,
A big soft snail is here,
The sap of each of the cows is here,
A thing better than honey and spruce,
A bogle yellow and fresh is here.

A thing better than right is here,
The fist of the big priest is here,
A thing better than the carcase is here,
The head of the dead man is here,
A thing better than wine is here,
The full of the cog of Caristine
Of live things soft and fair are here,
   Of live things soft and fair are here.

Come, thou churn, come;
Come, thou churn, come;
Come, thou life; come, thou breath;
Come, thou churn, come;
Come, thou churn, come;
Come, thou cuckoo; come, thou jackdaw;
Come, thou churn, come;
Come, thou churn, come;
Come will the little lark from the sky,
Come will the little carlin of the black-cap.

Come, thou churn, come;
Come, thou churn, come;
Come will the merle, come will the mavis,
Come will the music from the bower;
Come, thou churn, come;
Come, thou churn, come;
Come, thou wild cat,
To ease thy throat;
Come, thou churn, come;
Come, thou churn, come.

Come, thou hound, and quench thy thirst;
Come, thou churn, come;
Come, thou churn, come;
Come, thou poor; come, thou naked;
Come, thou churn, come;
Come, thou churn, come;
Come, ye alms-deserver
Of most distressful moan;
Come, thou churn, come;
Come, thou churn, come;
Come, each hungry creature,
And satisfy the thirst of thy body.

Come, thou churn, come;
Come, thou churn, come;
It is the God of the elements who bestowed on us,
And not the charm of a carlin with plant.
Come, thou churn, come;
Come, thou churn, come;
Come, thou fair-white Mary,
And endow to me my means;
Come, thou churn, come;
Come, thou churn, come;
Come, thou beauteous Bride,
And bless the substance of my kine.

Come, thou churn, come;
Come, thou churn, come;
The churning made of Mary,
In the fastness of the glen,
To decrease her milk,
To increase her butter;
Butter-milk to wrist,
Butter to elbow;
    Come, thou churn, come;
    Come, thou churn, come.

124

THE STORY OF NANGSA OBUM (Tibet)

*This translation of the story of Nangsa Obum, who was
empowered by the Goddess Tara, is a contemporary version of a
tradition Tibetan Folk Drama made by the Buddhist nun,
Tsultrim Allione. Tara is the female form of Buddha,
incarnation of the 'Moon of Wisdom', enlightened energy in the
female form. With the help of some of her friends and teachers,
Tsultrim Allione made this translation from a text that was
kept alive and passed down orally until it was recorded by
Marpa the Translator in the Eleventh Century. I have included
three extracts, filling in the story with a summary in prose.*

*After many years of devoted religious practice, Nangsa Obum's
parents conceived her in their old age. From birth she was a
remarkable child, compassionate and devoted to the Goddess
Tara whom she said had sent her into the world to help all
sentient beings. Nangsa was also extraordinarily beautiful, and
this worked against her, for although her only desire was to
spend her life practising the Dharma (the teachings of Buddha),
she soon had many suitors. Her parents sent all the suitors away
until one day she was spotted by a ruthless nobleman,
Dragchen, King of Rinang. In spite of her wishes, he tricked
and blackmailed her parents into forcing her to marry his son,
and her parents soon forgot the destiny for which she'd been
born. They were excited at the prospect of such a fine match for
their daughter. Nangsa begged to be released, but they sent her
away to the far province where King Dragchen lived, laden
with wedding gifts and a strong admonition to respect her
husband and father-in-law in all things, to wake at cockcrow
and be 'like a dog at the door, who is the last to sleep', to
work hard for everyone and never to think of herself.*

*After seven years of marriage Nangsa bore a beautiful son,
whom she named Lhau Darpo. She was much loved and
respected by all in the palace except her father-in-law's sister,
Ani Nyemo, who was jealous of her and made her life
miserable. Although he loved her, Nangsa's husband*

*wouldn't listen when she tried to tell him about Ani Nyemo,
and how she longed to go away and practise the Dharma. One
day in the fields Nangsa gave food to two yogis, disciples of the
saint Milarepa. As a result Ani Nyemo beat her, and told her
husband she had tried to seduce the yogis and was a whore. Her
husband believed his aunt and beat her severely, breaking three
ribs and covering her body with blood. The next day she was
visited by a manifestation of the great lama Sakya Gyaltsen,
who appeared to her in the form of a beggar. He talked to her
about the purifying effect of her suffering, and advised her to
come to him to practise the Dharma. When she heard the name
Sakya Gyaltsen, the hair stood up on her arms and tears came
to her eyes. But her father-in-law, passing her room at that
moment, saw her giving jewels to a beggar, beat her to the point
of death, and took away her son. That night she died of a
broken heart.*

*Her mind left her body like a hair being drawn from butter.
For seven days she remained dead, and saw hell, and the Lord
of Death, who sent her back into life to fulfil her destiny.
Flowers rained down from the sky, and she was surrounded by a
rainbow of light as she re-entered her body. Her family, when
they heard of the miracle of her return to life, begged her to come
back to them, but she explained that she had been sent back to
practise the Dharma. Then her little son climbed into her lap
and began to plead with her:*

A little boy like me without his mother
Is like a kingdom without a king;
A kingdom has no meaning without a king.
Please do not go away without me!

I am a little boy who has been separated from his
    mother,
I am like a young man with no courage.
Even if he talks very much,
He cannot protect his parents,
Or injure his enemies.
Think about this and do not leave me!

I am a little boy who has been separated from his
   mother,
Like a girl with no hair,
Even if she has many ornaments,
She will not get a husband.
Think of that and do not leave me!

I am a little boy who has been separated from his
   mother,
Like a horse that can run fast but cannot be controlled,
It cannot be sold.
Think of that and do not leave me!

I am a little boy who has been separated from his
   mother,
Like a mule with a weak back,
Even if it is fed well,
It is useless.
Think of that and do not leave me!

I am a little boy who has been separated from his
   mother,
Like a businessman with no money,
Even if he works hard he does not get anywhere!
Think of that and do not leave me!

I am a little boy who has been separated from his
   mother,
Like a Mani wheel with no blessings,
No one will bother with it.
Think of that and do not leave me!

I am a little boy who has been separated from his
   mother,
Like a bird without wings,
Even if it tries to fly it will fall down again and again,
Think of that and do not leave me!

I am a little boy who has been separated from his
    mother,
Like a place where there is no grass and no water,
People may come,
But they will not stay!
Think of that and do not leave me!

I am a little boy who has been separated from his
    mother,
I will be a leper, no one will want to be near me,
Without you I am like that!
So please think of that and do not leave me!
Please come back home!

*Nangsa, seeing her son in this state, felt sorry for him and
started to cry; but then she realised that if she went back to the
palace she would have further obstacles. So she put her hand on
his head and said:*

I was dead but I came back to life,
So you can be happy.
There is nothing and no one who does not die,
But there are few who die and come back to life.
It is difficult to be a delog.
Death may come at any time.

I am like a snow mountain,
And you are a snow lion,
Do not be attached to me!
I am just an ordinary snow mountain,
Unlike my husband who is a big one,
So I can be melted by the sun . . .
It is very dangerous.

You are a golden eagle,
Do not be attached to me,
I am just a small rocky hill,
I might get blown up by lightning.

You, a beautiful deer,
Do not be attached to me, I am like a grassy hill,
There are other, better meadows,
I am dangerously small when autumn comes.

You are a little golden fish,
Do not be attached to me,
I am like a small lake that may dry up in the sun,
There are big oceans that are safer.

You are a beautiful bird,
Do not be attached to me,
I am like a little garden that may dry up.
There are bigger gardens.

You are a beautiful golden bee,
Do not be attached to me,
I am just an ordinary flower.
There are big lotuses nearby.
I could be destroyed by hail.

My little son, do not be attached to me,
The delog Nangsa Obum.
The Rinang family is more secure,
I may die,
Listen to my words and keep them in your mind, Lhau
    Darpo!

Then he pleaded with his mother again, saying:

You who are caring for me very compassionately,
My only mother, listen to me, Lhau Darpo!

If my mother and father had not made
The seed of my being,
How could I become a rope pulling them into Samsara?

If I am a snow lion,
If I do not stay with you, the snow mountain,
Even if lightning does not kill me,
My blue mane won't grow,
So until I get my blue mane please stay!
After I get my blue mane we will both go to practise
   the Dharma.
Until that time the sun will not melt you,
You can stay in the shadows.

If I, who am like an eagle,
Staying on a high rocky mountain,
Am not connected to the mountain,
Even if I am not killed,
I will not grow my big wings.
So please wait until I am big enough to fly,
Then we will fly high in the sky and practise the
   Dharma.
Until then we will not be exploded by lightning,
Because we will get a powerful guru to protect us.

If a little deer like me,
Is not in a forest,
Even if it is not killed by hunters,
It won't get its beautiful horns.
So please do not go until I get my beautiful horns.
Then we will go together to practise the Dharma.
Until then hail will not destroy you,
Because we can tell the clouds to go elsewhere.

If a little fish like me,
Is not in you, the mother, water,
Even if the fisherman's hook does not catch me,
I will never be able to swim fast.
Until I get this strong body,
Please, mother lake, stay here!
When I am strong enough, you and I will practise the
    Dharma together.
Until then the sun won't dry you up,
Because we can pray to the nagas, who live under the
    water.

If a little songbird like me
Is not attached to a garden,
Even if an eagle does not kill me,
I will never get my beautiful voice.
So until I get my beautiful voice,
Please stay here,
Then we will go to practise the Dharma.
Until then you will not be dried up in the autumn,
Because we can tell time not to let this happen.

If a little bee like me,
Is not connected to you, the mother flower,
Even if birds do not kill me,
I will never get my silver wings.
Until I can make my own honey,
Please, wild flower, do not go away!
Until then you will not be destroyed by hail,
Because we will keep a magic vase to stop the hail.

If I, little Lhau Darpo,
Am not with you, the kind mother,
I will not grow up.
Until I can get along by myself,
Please do not leave me!
When I am big enough we can go together and practise
　　the Dharma.
You will not die before then, because we will do a
　　special initiation and pray to Amitabha, the deity
　　of long life.

If Ani Nyemo talked about you to my father,
Causing him to beat you,
Remember compassion is the most important thing in
　　Dharma, and do not be angry.
Your friendly little boy is crying, and if you do not
　　have compassion, and do not listen to me,
That is not Dharma, mother!

If you have compassion, even if you live in an ordinary
　　house,
You are practising the Dharma.
If you do not have compassion,
There is no difference between you,
And the wild animals who live in caves.

*Her son seemed so small and wise, and everyone was pleading
with her so much to return, that Nangsa decided to return to the
palace and teach her family the Dharma. But in spite of all that
had happened, she was still unable to turn their minds towards
the teaching of the Buddha. At last she begged them again to
allow her to go away and practise the Dharma. They refused,
but agreed to allow her to visit her parents, taking the child with
her to prevent her running away. In her parents' house Nangsa
found a piece of cloth she had left unfinished when she left
home. She decided to finish weaving it, using its images to teach
the Dharma to the friends who had gathered around her. Her*

mother ordered her to give up all ideas of practising the
Dharma, and be a housewife. Nangsa's answer was that she
could not do that until the sun stopped shining, and the moon
stopped waxing and waning. Her mother, taking her son from
her, threw ash in her face and turned her out of the house.

At last Nangsa, free of family and having lost her son, was
able to go to the lama Sakya Gyaltsen. At first she had great
trouble persuading him to accept her, since 'ordinary girls
cannot practise the Dharma', and he saw her beauty as a
further obstacle. Nangsa, becoming desperate, took a knife and
prepared to kill herself in his presence. Finally he accepted her
as a pupil and gave her the teaching she longed for. When her
family came to know what had happened, her husband
gathered a great army and attacked the monastery of Sakya
Gyaltsen. The guru allowed himself to be captured, and then
moved mountains and revived the dead to demonstrate the
powerlessness of the king's army. After that he invited Nangsa
to show her powers so that all would become devoted to her. She
made her shawl into wings, flew up into the air and sang this
song:

You, father and son and the rest of you, listen to me!
Listen to Nangsa Obum!
You have tried to make a snow lion into a dog,
But this is impossible!
Now I am on the snow mountain showing my mane!
You tried to tame a wild yak and turn it into a cow,
But this is impossible,
That is why I did not stay with you.
Now I am showing off my horns!
You tried to saddle the wild mule who lives in the
    forest,
That is why I ran away.
Now I am showing you my power.

You tried to make a wild bird into a hen,
But you cannot do that,
That is why I am in the forest showing off my plumage.
You tried to make a rainbow into a piece of cloth,
This is impossible,
Though it is visible it is not a concrete substance.
Now I show you this power.
You tried to make a delicate cloud into a cloth,
You could not so that is why I am staying here.
Now the cloud is showing you its capacity to make
    rain.
You tried to make a wild monkey into a servant,
But this is impossible.
Now I am showing you how I can climb!
You tried to make the delog Nangsa Obum into a wife,
But even though you put tsendura into my hair parting,
You cannot hold me.
Here I am, flying above you,
I have flown to Tsari,
I have some bamboo from Tsari to prove it!
Like a yak that has worked hard plowing,
Now I show you the furrows.
If I want to fly like an eagle,
I fly like this!
If I want to dive like a hawk,
I do it this way!

The royal family and the soldiers were all converted. Nangsa's husband, her father-in-law and even the bad Ani Nyemo left worldly life to practise the Dharma. Her son became king and ruled virtuously, following the Dharma. Everyone in the kingdom followed the Dharma carefully.

Nangsa Obum stayed in the mountains, leaving her thighprint and footprint in many places, as though stone were butter.

134

NOTE:
A *Delog* is one who has died and come back to life.
Samsara is the concern with worldly things that
prevents us from growing spiritually.
The *Dharma* is the way and teachings of Buddha.
A *Mani Wheel* is a prayer wheel.

Acknowledgments

The editor and publishers gratefully acknowledge permission from the following to reprint the poems in this book:

'The Song of The Broken Reeds' by Ingrid Jonker, translated by J. Cope and William Plomer, from *Selected Poems* (Human and Rousseau Publishers, Cape Town, 1988); 'Invocation' and 'Spell of Creation' by Kathleen Raine from *Selected Poems* (Hamish Hamilton, 1956); 'The Child' by P. K. Page from *Evening Dance of The Gray Flies* (Oxford University Press, Canada, 1981); 'The Mirage' and 'A Lecture to the Flat Earth Society' by Gwendolyn MacEwan from *Earthlight* (General Publishing Co., Canada, 1982); 'Return from Arvon' by Meg Easten; extracts from 'Insomnia' and 'Poems for Blok' by Marina Tsvetayeva, translated by Elaine Feinstein, from *Selected Poems*, (Hutchinson, 1977); 'The World has Passed', 'The Lion from Rio', 'The Conceiving' and 'Giving Birth' by Penelope Shuttle from the collections *The Orchard Upstairs* and *The Lion from Rio* (Oxford University Press, 1980 and 1986); extract from 'Old Woman' by Cam Hubert; 'Ends Meet' by Frances Bellerby from *Selected Poems* (Enitharmon Press, 1971): 'All the words' by Gillian Hanscombe and Suniti Namjoshi from *Dancing The Tightrope* (The Women's Press, 1987); heart note by Gillian Allnutt; 'Praise Song for My Mother' by Grace Nichols from *The Fat Black Woman's Poems* (Virago Press, 1984); 'The Wound' by Louise Glück from her collection *Firstborn* (Ecco Press, New York, 1968); 'In Celebration of My Uterus' by Anne Sexton with permission of The Peters Fraser & Dunlop Group Ltd., New York; 'A Vision' by Denise Levertov from *Selected Poems* (Bloodaxe Books, 1986) by permission of the New Directions Publishing Corporation; 'Into the Hour' by Elizabeth Jennings from *Collected Poems* (Carcanet, 1987); 'The Sleeper of The Rowan Tree' from *A Northumbrian Sequence* by Kathleen Raine from *Selected Poems* (Hamish Hamilton, 1956); 'Remember?' by Alice Walker from *Horses Make a Landscape More Beautiful* (The Women's Press, 1985); 'Wind a Change' by Grace Nichols from her collection *i is a long memoried woman* (Caribbean Cultural International, 1983); 'Kitchen Murder' by Pat Lowther from *A Stone Diary* © (Oxford University Press, Canada, 1977); 'No Dialects Please' by Merle Collins from *Watchers and Seekers* (The

Women's Press, 1987); 'No Regrets' by Patricia Hilaire from
A Dangerous Knowing (Sheba Feminist Publishers, 1985);
'Calderpark Zoo Song' by Liz Lochhead from *True
Confessions* (Edinburgh University Press, 1985); 'Do a Dance
for Daddy' by Fran Landesman from *In the Pink* (The
Women's Press, 1983) and *Invade My Privacy* (Cape, 1978);
'Rotting Song' by Libby Houston from *Plain Clothes* (Alison
and Busby, 1971); 'Not Waving But Drowning', 'Egocentric'
and 'Happiness' by Stevie Smith from *The Collected Poems of
Stevie Smith* (Penguin Modern Classics) by permission of
J MacGibbon (executor); extracts from 'Overheard in County
Sligo' by Gillian Clarke from *Selected Poems* (Carcanet Press
Ltd., 1985); 'The Surgeon at 2am' by Sylvia Plath from
Crossing The Water (Faber & Faber, 1971); 'Watching Dark
Circle' by Denise Levertov from *Oblique Prayers* (Bloodaxe
Books, 1986); 'Muse', 'Reading Hamlet' and 'Lot's Wife', by
Anna Akhmatova, translated by D.M. Thomas, from *Way of
all the Earth* (Secker & Warburg, 1979), and 'Epilogue' by
Anna Akhmatova, translated by D.M. Thomas, from *Requiem
and Poem Without A Hero* (Elek Books, 1976) with permission
of Secker & Warburg; 'The Woman Who Wanted To Be A
Hero' and 'Poem on the Day of the Autumn Equinox' by
Michèle Roberts from *The Mirror of The Mother* (Methuen);
'Baby-Sitting' by Gillian Clarke from *Selected Poems*
(Carcanet Press Ltd., 1985); 'The Woman Who Could Not
Live With Her Faulty Heart' by Margaret Atwood from
Selected Poems 11: Poems Selected And New 1976-1986 ©
Margaret Atwood 1986, by permission of Oxford University
Press, Canada; 'Some People's Dreams Pay All Their Bills' by
Irina Ratushinskaya, translated by David McDuff, from *No,
I'm Not Afraid* (Bloodaxe Books, 1986); 'About Death' by
P.K. Page from *Evening Dance of The Gray Flies* (Oxford
University Press, Canada, 1981); 'Romney's Proposal' from
Aurora Leigh by Elizabeth Barrett Browning (The Women's
Press, 1978); 'Goblin Market' by Christina Rossetti from *A
Choice of Christina Rossetti's Verse* (Faber & Faber, 1975); a
selection of work from Emily Dickinson from *The Complete
Poems of Emily Dickinson* (Faber & Faber, 1972); 'The Charm
of the Churn' as recited by Mary MacLeillan from *Carmina
Gadelica* (Scottish Academic Press, Edinburgh 1972); the
chapter 'The Story of Nangsa Obum' from *Women of Wisdom*
by Tsultrim Allione (Arkana, 1984).